DK Pocket Eyewitness

ROCKS AND MINERALS

FACTS AT YOUR FINGERTIPS

LONDON, NEW YORK, MUNICH,
MELBOURNE, and DELHI

DK DELHI
Project editor Bharti Bedi
Project art editor Deep Shikha Walia
Senior editor Kingshuk Ghoshal
Senior art editor Govind Mittal
Assistant art editor Aanchal Singal
DTP designers Rajesh Singh Adhikari,
Jaypal Singh Chauhan
Picture researcher Sumedha Chopra
Managing editor Saloni Talwar
Managing art editor Romi Chakraborty
CTS manager Balwant Singh
Production manager Pankaj Sharma

DK LONDON
Senior editor Fleur Star
Senior art editor Philip Letsu
Jacket editor Manisha Majithia
Jacket designer Laura Brim
Jacket design development manager
Sophia Tampakopolous
Production editor Ben Marcus
Production controller Mary Slater

Publisher Andrew Macintyre
Associate publishing director Liz Wheeler
Art director Phil Ormerod
Publishing director Jonathan Metcalf

Consultant Kevin Walsh

First published in Great Britain in 2012
by Dorling Kindersley Limited
80 Strand, London WC2R 0RL

**Discover more at
www.dk.com**

CONTENTS

Scales and sizes
This book contains profiles of rocks and minerals with scale drawings to indicate their size.

15 cm
(6 in)

Our rocky planet

Our planet is like an onion, made up of a number of layers. In the centre is a solid core, which is surrounded by the mantle and the crust. We live on Earth's surface on top of the crust, the thin outer layer that carries oceans and continents. These layers developed early in Earth's history. During Earth's formation, denser materials, such as iron, sank to the centre, while lighter materials, such as silicates and other minerals, rose to the surface.

Upper mantle is made of warm, mobile rocks

Core and mantle

The core is made up of a solid inner part and a liquid outer part. The mantle is a layer of dense minerals, just above the core. High pressure makes the lower mantle solid, while the minerals in the upper mantle are like a gluey liquid. Molten rocks found inside Earth are called magma.

Lower mantle contains dense rock formed under pressure

Outer core creates Earth's magnetic field as the molten material moves

Inner core is solid and contains a mixture of iron and nickel

Atmosphere consists of gases

Crust is made of solid rock, and forms oceans and continents

The oldest type of rock is Acasta gneiss, which first formed 4.2 billion years ago.

Lava flowing today from Kilauea volcano, Hawaiian Islands, will cool to form igneous rocks.

How old are rocks?

Rocks formed when Earth was cool enough for them to become solid. The first rock on Earth solidified around 4.2 billion years ago. Rocks and minerals have been forming ever since and are still forming today – at Earth's surface, in the crust, on the ocean floor, and in the mantle deep below.

Earth's crust

The crust is made up of "panels" called tectonic plates. When two plates collide, they push against one another, sometimes forming mountains. This tectonic movement may bring up rocks from deep inside the mantle to the surface.

Eurasian plate

Boundary between the two plates, where the Himalayan mountains formed

Indian plate

There are around 12 large tectonic plates on Earth's crust, both on land and below the seas and oceans.

What is a mineral?

Green chrysocolla is a mineral

A mineral is a naturally occurring, solid inorganic substance, which means it doesn't come from the remains of plants or animals. It is made from chemical elements – simple substances that cannot be broken down further. Minerals grow or cement together to form rocks.

What is a mineral made of?

Minerals are chemical compounds made up of two or more chemical elements. The atoms in the elements bind together to form solid pieces called crystals. Some crystals can grow to several metres wide, but others are so tiny they can only be seen with a microscope.

When crystals have enough room to grow, they form **well-defined shapes**, such as seen in this amethyst.

Weak bond

Graphite structure

Carbon atoms

Strong bond

Diamond structure

Pattern of atoms

The atoms of elements in a mineral form a se[...] pattern that never changes. This pattern give[...] the mineral its properties, such as hardness, colour, and shape. For example, graphite and diamond are both forms of carbon. In graphit[...] the atoms are linked with weak bonds, which makes it soft. Diamond has strong bonds, making it the hardest mineral.

Feldspar in granite

Rock-forming minerals

Mineralogists (people who study minerals) sometimes group minerals into two types: ore minerals and rock-forming minerals. This group includes feldspar, which is one of the most abundant of all minerals and is found in many types of rock.

Ore minerals

Some minerals are mined for their metal content. Known as ore minerals, they are crushed and separated and then refined and melted to produce metal. This LKAB mine in Sweden is the largest in the world. Most of its ore is magnetite, which is used to produce iron.

MINERAL OR NOT?

Oil rig, North Sea

Although some substances such as **oil** may be called minerals, they come from the remains of living things and are actually classified as hydrocarbons.

Minerals such as rubies, diamonds, and emeralds can be copied and produced in laboratories. Such artificial versions are not true minerals because they do not grow naturally.

Artificial rubies

What is a rock?

A rock is a solid collection of mineral grains that grow or become cemented together. Geologists (people who study rocks and minerals) classify rocks into three main types on the basis of how they are formed – igneous, sedimentary, and metamorphic.

Composition

Every rock is made up of one or more minerals. For example, gabbro, an igneous rock, is made up of minerals including olivine, pyroxene, and plagioclase feldspar.

Plagioclase feldspar
The light grains are a type of feldspar called plagioclase. There are different kinds of feldspar minerals, which form part of most types of rock.

Gabbro

Olivine
This mineral forms only in igneous rocks that solidify below the ground. It contains iron and magnesium.

Thin slice of gabbro seen under a microscope

Pyroxene
This mineral is abundant in Earth's mantle. Some rocks on the Moon are also made of pyroxene.

TYPES OF ROCK

Igneous rocks form from molten magma that has cooled and hardened on or below Earth's surface.

Obsidian is an igneous rock

Red colour due to iron oxide

Sedimentary rocks form at Earth's surface and consist of layers of rock fragments, minerals, or organic matter such as sea shells that have been deposited on top of each other.

Red sandstone is a sedimentary rock

Metamorphic rocks can form when rocks are squeezed by pressure and heated deep under Earth's crust.

Banded gneiss is a metamorphic rock

Be a collector

Rocks and minerals can be found everywhere – up in the mountains, along streams, on beaches, and even on a driveway! Collecting them and recording the finds is a popular hobby that dates back to the 19th century.

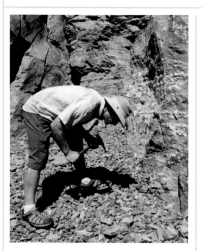

Safety first

Protective clothing and shoes may need to be worn at certain collection sites. Rocks can splinter while chipping or trimming, so it is best to wear protective goggles and gloves. A compass and a map are useful for directions.

Map and compass

In the field

Before going out in the field to collect rocks, it is a good idea to find out about the site and the kind of specimens expected to be found there. Joining a group of collectors can be more fun and is safer than taking the trip alone.

Protective gloves

Hard ha

Goggles

Paint brush for cleaning specimens

Sieve for sorting rocks from sand

Trowel for digging soft rocks

Geological hammer with a rubber grip

Pocket knife

Wide-ended chisel for splitting rocks

ssential tools

ile collecting rocks and minerals in the field, a ge of tools are required. These include a chisel d a geological hammer. A regular hammer may linter the rock or the mineral specimen dangerously.

eeping records

some cases, it is better to observe and record mples with a camera or in a sketchpad than nove them from a site, which may damage the cks. The exact location and details of a find n be recorded in a notebook.

Notebook for noting specimen details

Digital camera

Bubble wrap to carry specimens

Handle with care

To collect a sample of a rock or a mineral, chip or trim it to size with a hammer. Wrap it in a newspaper or a bubble wrap to keep it scratch-free.

Cleaning specimens

Most specimens are dirty when collected. Surplus rock fragments can be removed from a specimen by washing in water. A gentle scrub with a brush helps remove loose soil and debris when the specimen is dry. Every specimen must be cleaned only as much as needed. It is best to begin with the most gentle method.

Cleaning tools include tweezers, toothbrushes, and even dental picks

Index cards to list specimens alphabetically and store field notes or other details

Labelling

After the specimens have been identified, label them for future reference, along with notes on their location or other specific details.

Magnifying glass to study and identify r

Cotton to clean specimens

Plastic box
for brittle pieces

Storage and display

To avoid damage, specimens can be stored in individual trays or boxes. It is useful to keep an index for larger collections, using index cards to record details of the specimens, such as their locations and the dates of collection.

Templates to make cardboard boxes for storage

Rocks

When minerals grow or cement together, they can form rocks. Some rocks, such as dolomite, are made up of only one mineral. However, most rocks are a combination of two or more minerals. Some also contain fossils of plants and animals. New rocks form in different ways – when magma becomes solid, when old rocks break down, or when there is a change in temperature or pressure.

MOAI
Found on Easter Island, the Moai are human figures carved out of pieces of rock called tuff.

How rocks are made

Rocks are formed and destroyed all the time. There are three main ways rocks form. Igneous rocks form when magma and lava solidify. Sedimentary rocks form in layers made up of pieces of existing rock that have been broken down by erosion and weathering. Metamorphic rocks form by heat or pressure.

Pluton shape forms when magma cools in a mass

When magma comes to surface it is called **lava**

Sill shape form when magma cools between rock layers

Earth's crust

Igneous rocks

Igneous rocks form when hot, liquid magma inside Earth cools and becomes solid. When this happens below ground, the rocks are called "intrusive". They can form in three shapes – pluton, dyke, and sill. When magma comes to the surface as lava and cools above ground, the rocks are called "extrusive".

Magma chamber deep within Earth's crust

Dyke shape forms when magma breaks through existing rock structures

THE ROCK CYCLE

Rocks are either igneous, sedimentary, or metamorphic. Over thousands of years, rocks can change from one type to another, from igneous to sedimentary to metamorphic and back to igneous. This process is called the rock cycle.

Erosion

Sedimentary rock

Burial

Igneous rock

Metamorph rock

Melting

edimentary rocks

dimentary rocks form on, or
ry near, Earth's surface where
oded rock particles
ansported by wind,
ater, and ice are
posited on dry
d, on the beds
rivers and lakes,
d in the seas.

Weathering produces
sediments that are
carried by rivers

Sediments
may deposit
on the sea bed

Pieces of rock carried by water
and wind get deposited as layers
called **strata**. Over years these
pieces, or sediments, cement
together to form rocks.

Layers of rock

etamorphic rocks

isting rocks can change due to heat or pressure,
both. During this long process, new minerals
ow from the chemicals in the old
cks, forming new rocks.

Rocks can change due to the
pressure of movement in
Earth's crust. This is called
dynamic pressure. It can also
cause cracks called **faults.**

Fault

hen the heat from magma
akes" surrounding rock
that it changes, it is
lled **thermal contact.**

Earth's crust

**Magma
chamber**

Rocks deep in the crust can change due to the
eat and pressure caused by the weight of the
ocks above. This is called **regional change.**

Layers of rock

Identifying rocks

Geologists can identify rocks through characteristics such as the size, shape, and arrangement of their grains. Grains in igneous rock are usually randomly arranged. Sedimentary rocks are made of rock particles and minerals that are cemented together. In metamorphic rocks, the grains are often aligned into patterns, known as foliations.

IGNEOUS ROCK CHARACTERISTICS

Peridotite

Basalt

Pink granite

Large grains

Igneous rocks form below ground when magma in Earth's crust solidifies. The grains are well-developed and large as they have enough time to grow. Peridotite is an igneous rock with well-developed grains.

Small grains

When magma erupts from volcanoes and reaches Earth's surface, it is called lava. When this lava solidifies above the ground, it cools down rapidly. This gives little time for grains to develop. Basalt is an example of an igneous rock with small grains.

Colour

The mineral content of an igneous rock can be determined from its colour. A light-coloured igneous rock, such as pink granite, is rich in silica. Dark-coloured rocks have less silica but contain other dark, heavy minerals.

EDIMENTARY ROCK HARACTERISTICS

Grain size

The grains in sedimentary rocks are of different sizes and textures. Conglomerate grains are coarse.

Conglomerate

Grain shape

The shape of particles in sedimentary rocks show how the particles were transported. The particles of this sandstone were rounded by desert winds.

Millet-seed sandstone

Presence of fossils

The presence of fossils is an indicator of rock type. They are very common in sedimentary rocks such as limestone, but rare in metamorphic rocks. Fossils never occur in igneous rocks.

Freshwater limestone

METAMORPHIC ROCK CHARACTERISTICS

Fine grain size

Marble

Size of grains

Grains in metamorphic rocks grow slowly. Large grains indicate that the rock was formed under high pressure and heat. Rocks that form under lower pressure and heat have smaller grains.

Crinkled layers

Folded schist

Foliation

When a metamorphic rock forms under pressure, its grains may line up in patterns. This gives the rock a distinct wavy appearance.

Igneous rocks

The Latin word *ignis* means "fire". Igneous rocks form when hot, molten magma inside Earth is pushed towards the crust and cools above or below the surface, forming solid rocks.

FOCUS ON...
FORMATION
Igneous rocks form some amazing natura structures, and man-made ones too.

Obsidian

Obsidian forms when lava cools so rapidly that mineral crystals do not have time to grow. In ancient times, Native Americans, Aztecs, and Greeks used obsidian to make weapons, tools, and ornaments.

WHERE FORMED	Above ground
SHAPE WHEN FORMED	Lava flow
GRAIN SIZE	Fine
COLOUR	Black, brown
MINERAL CONTENT	Glass

Basalt

When the lava cools and solidifies into basalt on Earth's surface, it may split into many-sided columns. Basalt forms ocean floors and large outcrops on land, such as the Deccan Traps, in India. It is rich in iron and magnesium.

WHERE FORMED	Above ground
SHAPE WHEN FORMED	Lava flow
GRAIN SIZE	Fine to coarse
COLOUR	Dark grey to black
MINERAL CONTENT	Pyroxene, plagioclase, olivine, magnetite

The Giant's Causeway, Northern Ireland, is ~,000 basalt pillars cked closely together.

▲ The Devil's Tower, made of phonolite, was declared a national monument of the USA in 1906.

▲ Sierra Nevada is a huge mass of granite, formed at great depth, brought to the surface.

▲ Mount Rushmore's granite has been carved to show the faces of American presidents.

Granite

Granite is formed deep inside Earth's crust. It forms when magma cools down slowly. Crushed granite is used as gravel and road-building material. Polished granite is used for kitchen worktops and gravestones.

WHERE FORMED Below ground

SHAPE WHEN FORMED Pluton

GRAIN SIZE Medium to coarse

COLOUR White, light grey, grey, pink, red

MINERAL CONTENT Feldspars, quartz, mica, hornblende

Dolerite

Dolerite is an extremely hard rock and occurs in fissures in other rocks. You can see the crystals in dolerite with the naked eye.

WHERE FORMED Below ground

SHAPE WHEN FORMED Dykes, sills

GRAIN SIZE Fine to medium

COLOUR Dark grey to black, often mottled white

MINERAL CONTENT Plagioclase, pyroxene, quartz, magnetite, olivine

Diorite

A prized rock in ancient Egypt, diorite was used to build columns, figures, and sarcophagi (stone coffins), and for lining the chambers of some pyramids.

WHERE FORMED   Below ground

SHAPE WHEN FORMED   Pluton, dyke, sill

GRAIN SIZE   Medium to coarse

COLOUR   Mottled black, dark green, grey, white

MINERAL CONTENT   Plagioclase, hornblende, biotite

Rhyolite

Kimberlite

Kimberlite is the major source of diamonds. Kimberley in South Africa was one of the first sites to be mined for diamonds and inspired the name of the rock. However, not every occurrence yields gem-quality diamonds.

WHERE FORMED   Below ground

SHAPE WHEN FORMED   Dyke, pipe

GRAIN SIZE   Fine to coarse

COLOUR   Dark grey

MINERAL CONTENT   Olivine, pyroxene, mica, garnet, ilmenite, diamond

Rhyolite is a rare rock that forms from volcanic eruptions. Its lava is very rich in silica, so it is very sticky and may plug the volcano's vent.

WHERE FORMED   Above ground

SHAPE WHEN FORMED   Lava flow

GRAIN SIZE   Fine to coarse

COLOUR   Very light to medium grey, light pink

MINERAL CONTENT   Quartz, potassium feldspar, glass, biotite, amphibole, plagioclase

Peridotite

This rock forms much of Earth's mantle. Eruptions of magma from the mantle can bring up nodules (lumps) of peridotite to the surface. It is a major source of chromium.

Green olivine

WHERE FORMED   Below ground

SHAPE WHEN FORMED   Pluton, dyke, sill

GRAIN SIZE   Coarse

COLOUR   Dark green to black

MINERAL CONTENT   Olivine, pyroxene, garnet, chromite

Andesite

This rock is named after the Andes mountains of South America. It erupts from volcanoes and is found in areas where one tectonic plate slides under another, such as in the Andes.

WHERE FORMED   Above ground

SHAPE WHEN FORMED   Lava flow

GRAIN SIZE   Fine, with some small grains

COLOUR   Light to dark grey, reddish-pink

MINERAL CONTENT   Feldspars, pyroxene, amphibole, biotite

Pumice

Highly porous and frothlike, pumice forms when gas-filled liquid magma erupts like a fizzy drink from a shaken bottle and cools quickly. The resulting foam solidifies into a rock that is light enough to float on water.

WHERE FORMED	Above ground
SHAPE WHEN FORMED	Lava flow
GRAIN SIZE	Fine
COLOUR	White, yellow, grey, black
MINERAL CONTENT	Glass, feldspar, quartz

Ignimbrite

This is a type of tuff that is deposited by flowing rivers of ash. Such flows can cause deaths during volcanic eruptions. In June 1912, Novarupta, a volcano in Alaska, produced the largest quantity of ignimbrite in history.

WHERE FORMED	Above ground
SHAPE WHEN FORMED	Lava flow
GRAIN SIZE	Fine
COLOUR	Pale cream, red-brown, grey
MINERAL CONTENT	Igneous rock and crystal fragments, welded volcanic glass

Pélé's hair

Named after the Hawaiian goddess of fire, this rock has a fine, wispy texture. It forms when very liquid magma is spewed out from a volcano and cools rapidly in mid-air.

WHERE FORMED	Above ground
SHAPE WHEN FORMED	Lava spray
GRAIN SIZE	Very fine
COLOUR	Pale brown
MINERAL CONTENT	Basaltic glass

Tuff

Tuff forms when foaming magma comes up to the surface as a mixture of hot gases and glowing particles, and is thrown out from a volcano.

WHERE FORMED Above ground

SHAPE WHEN FORMED Lava flow

GRAIN SIZE Fine

COLOUR Grey, brown, green

MINERAL CONTENT Glassy, crystalline fragments

Syenite

Syenite is an attractive, multi-coloured rock, which may be polished and used as a decorative stone. It forms large crystals as it cools slowly underground. It looks similar to granite but unlike granite, it contains little, if any, quartz.

WHERE FORMED Below ground

SHAPE WHEN FORMED Pluton, dyke, sill

GRAIN SIZE Medium to coarse

COLOUR Grey, pink, red

MINERAL CONTENT Potassium feldspar, plagioclase, biotite, amphibole, pyroxene, feldspathoids

Dacite

Dacite derives its name from Dacia, a territory in the Roman Empire, where it was first described. It forms part of several volcanoes, such as the one at Crater Lake, Oregon, USA.

WHERE FORMED Above ground

SHAPE WHEN FORMED Pluton, dyke, sill

GRAIN SIZE Fine

COLOUR Grey to black

MINERAL CONTENT Plagioclase, quartz, pyroxene, amphibole, biotite

Anorthosite

The ancient light-coloured highlands on the far side of the Moon are made of anorthosite. It forms large masses or layers between rocks such as gabbro and peridotite.

WHERE FORMED Below ground

SHAPE WHEN FORMED Lava flow

GRAIN SIZE Medium to coarse

COLOUR Light grey to white

MINERAL CONTENT Plagioclase, olivine, pyroxene, magnetite

rachyte

he name "trachyte" comes from the ireek word for "rough". This tough and esistant rock has been used for paving bads for thousands of years.

WHERE FORMED   Above ground
SHAPE WHEN FORMED   Lava flow, dyke, sill
GRAIN SIZE   Fine to medium
COLOUR   Off-white, grey, pale yellow, pink
MINERAL CONTENT
anidine, plagioclase, eldspathoids, quartz, livine, pyroxene, biotite

Rhomb porphyry

'orphyry refers to gneous rocks with arge-grained rystals. Rhomb orphyry gets its ame from the hombic, or liamond, shape f its large crystals.

WHERE FORMED   Above ground
SHAPE WHEN FORMED   Lava flow, dyke, sill
GRAIN SIZE   Medium
COLOUR   Grey-white, red-brown, purple
MINERAL CONTENT   Feldspar

Pegmatite

Pegmatite is one of the sources of important ore minerals, which provide useful metals such as tungsten. Pegmatites are also important sources of some gemstones, and mica.

WHERE FORMED   Below ground
SHAPE WHEN FORMED   Pluton
GRAIN SIZE   Very coarse
COLOUR   Pink, white, cream
MINERAL CONTENT   Quartz, feldspar, mica, tourmaline, topaz

The Devil's Tower is **sacred** to many Native American Plains tribes, who call it "Bear's Tipi"

DEVIL'S TOWER
The Devil's Tower in Wyoming, USA, is a giant structure of phonolite, an igneous rock. It formed when a volcano erupted and the magma cooled and solidified to form underground columns. Over millions of years, its surrounding layers weathered away, leaving the columns exposed.

Sedimentary rocks

Sedimentary rocks make up 80–90 per cent of the rocks on Earth's surface. These rocks form on land when sediments or grains join together. They may be carried by wind or water to the sea where they are buried and form layers of rock.

▲ Chalk was used to make the first white colouring for art.

▲ Clay was often used by early artists for extracting the colour brown.

Limestone

Fine texture

Fossil of shell

Limestone forms in warm, shallow seas and is made of the mineral calcite, which comes from sea water or the shells and skeletons of sea animals. It is used as a building stone and as a raw material in manufacturing glass. On burning it produces lime, which is used to make cement.

ORIGIN	Sea bed
GRAIN SIZE	Fine to medium, angular to rounded
COLOUR	White, grey, pink
MINERAL CONTENT	Calcite
FOSSILS	Marine and freshwater invertebrates, plants

Rock gypsum

Also known as gyprock,
rock gypsum forms when
water evaporates from
oceans or salty lakes.
It is used as a
fertilizer and
to make
plaster board.

ORIGIN Sea bed
GRAIN SIZE
Medium to fine
crystalline
COLOUR White, pinkish, yellowish, grey
MINERAL CONTENT Gypsum
FOSSILS None

Dolomite

Dolomite rock is formed entirely of the
mineral dolomite. The Swiss Alps in Italy,
also known as the Dolomites, are almost
entirely composed of this rock.

*Compact
carbonate
rock*

ORIGIN Land
GRAIN SIZE Fine to
medium, crystalline
COLOUR Grey to
yellowish-grey
MINERAL CONTENT
Dolomite
FOSSILS
Invertebrates

Rock salt

Rock salt forms when
salty water evaporates.
As well as being used in
kitchens as table salt, it is
used to make soaps and
baking soda, among
other things.

ORIGIN Sea bed
GRAIN SIZE Coarse to fine crystalline
COLOUR White, orange-brown, blue
MINERAL CONTENT Halite
FOSSILS None

Chalk

Chalk is made up of the mineral
calcite, which comes from the shells and
skeletons of sea animals. The grains in chalk
are so small that they cannot be seen without
a magnifying glass.

ORIGIN Sea bed
GRAIN SIZE Very fine,
angular to rounded
COLOUR White,
grey, buff
**MINERAL
CONTENT** Calcite
FOSSILS
Invertebrates,
vertebrates

Peat

As plants decay over thousands of years, they slowly turn into coal. The formation of peat is the first step in this process. Peat forms in warm, moist climates, where there are enough nutrients, bacteria, and oxygen.

ORIGIN	Land
GRAIN SIZE	Medium, fine
COLOUR	Dark brown to black
MINERAL CONTENT	Carbon
FOSSILS	Plants, invertebrates

Anthracite

This form of coal contains a lot of carbon. It is glassy and cleaner to handle than other forms. Anthracite burns at a high temperature, with a blue flame, and produces very little smoke. It can be polished to make decorative items.

ORIGIN Land

GRAIN SIZE Fine

COLOUR Shiny black

MINERAL CONTENT
Carbon

FOSSILS Plants

ravertine

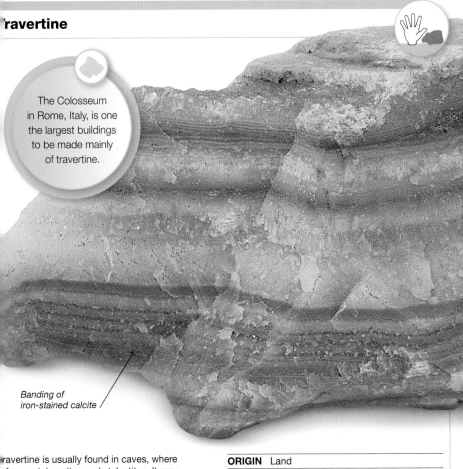

The Colosseum in Rome, Italy, is one the largest buildings to be made mainly of travertine.

Banding of iron-stained calcite

ravertine is usually found in caves, where forms stalagmites and stalactites. It may e formed by the evaporation of hot springs. he rock contains a pure form of calcium arbonate, and is often polished and used or walls and interior decorations.

ORIGIN	Land
GRAIN SIZE	Crystalline
COLOUR	Creamy white
MINERAL CONTENT	Calcite
FOSSILS	Rare

Chert

This rock is so hard, it can't be scratched with a knife. In the Stone Age, it was used for making tools and weapons. Today, chert is used in building roads, and can even be polished to make jewellery.

ORIGIN Sea bed, or as nodules in limestone

GRAIN SIZE Fine, crystalline

COLOUR Greyish

MINERAL CONTENT Chalcedony

FOSSILS Invertebrates, plants

Loess

The German word *loess* means "loose" and refers to the loose deposits of this rock by glacial winds. Loess is soft and crumbly and contains few clay minerals, so it feels smooth, not sticky, when wet.

ORIGIN Land

GRAIN SIZE
Very fine

COLOUR Yellowish or brownish

MINERAL CONTENT
Quartz, feldspar

FOSSILS Rare

Tufa

Tufa is formed when lime-rich water evaporates, leaving behind calcium carbonate. It gets deposited on cliffs, caves, and rock surfaces in regions where rainfall is low. In the process of formation, some pebbles and grains of sediment also get caught in it.

Flint

In prehistoric times, people used flakes of flint to make sharp-edged weapons including knives, scrapers, and arrowheads. Flint is a hard substance, rich in silica, and it is found as bands in limestone.

ORIGIN Nodules in limestone or dolomite
GRAIN SIZE Fine, crystalline
COLOUR Grey
MINERAL CONTENT Chalcedony
FOSSILS Invertebrates

Feldspathic gritstone

This rock is made up of sand-sized grains and gravel. Iron oxides may help bind the grains together.

Feldspar grain

ORIGIN Sea bed, land
GRAIN SIZE Coarse to medium, angular
COLOUR Brownish with a tinge of pink
MINERAL CONTENT Quartz, feldspar, mica
FOSSILS Invertebrates, vertebrates, plants

Tufa towers form underwater and can reach heights of more than 9 m (30 ft).

ORIGIN Land
GRAIN SIZE Fine, crystalline
COLOUR White or orange-stained
MINERAL CONTENT Calcite or silica
FOSSILS Rare

Shale

Shale is a highly fissile rock, meaning it breaks up into thin sheets. It forms from fine muds in various environments. Some shales have important deposits of oil in them.

ORIGIN Sea bed, freshwater, glacier

GRAIN SIZE Fine

COLOUR Grey

MINERAL CONTENT Clays, quartz, calcite

FOSSILS Invertebrates, vertebrates, plants

Breccia

Sandstone

Gaps between grains form different textures

Sandstones are classified by their different textures, which form from the way the sand-sized grains are cemented together. It is used as a building stone as it is durable.

ORIGIN Land

GRAIN SIZE Fine to medium, angular to rounded

COLOUR Cream to red

MINERAL CONTENT Quartz, feldspar

FOSSILS Vertebrates, invertebrates, plants

Breccia is a rock made up of generally large, rough grains cemented together. The lack of rounded grains shows that the rocks have not been transported far.

ORIGIN Sea bed, freshwater, glacier

GRAIN SIZE Very coarse, angular

COLOUR Varies

MINERAL CONTENT Any hard mineral can be present

FOSSILS Very rare

Conglomerate

Rocks that lie in water for a very long time become smooth and rounded. When these rocks are held together by cement, they form a conglomerate and may get transported long distances. Pebbles are the small rocks; cobbles are medium-sized rocks; and boulders are large. All these are larger than 2 mm (0.8 in) in size.

ORIGIN Sea bed, freshwater, glacier

GRAIN SIZE Very coarse, rounded

COLOUR Varies

MINERAL CONTENT Any hard mineral can be present

FOSSILS Very rare

rkose

This granitelike form of sandstone is different from other sandstones as it has more feldspar. It has a rough texture and its grains are usually cemented together by calcite.

RIGIN Sea bed, freshwater

RAIN SIZE Medium, angular

OLOUR Pinkish to pale grey

IINERAL CONTENT Quartz, feldspar

OSSILS Rare

Ironstone

Sandstones and limestones with more than 15 per cent iron content are called ironstones. These ancient rocks formed when there was not as much oxygen in the atmosphere as today.

ORIGIN Sea bed or land

GRAIN SIZE Fine to medium, crystalline to angular, oolitic

COLOUR Red, black, grey, striped

MINERAL CONTENT Hematite, goethite, chamosite, magnetite, siderite, limonite, jasper

FOSSILS Invertebrates

Clay

Clay grains are so fine that they can't even be seen with a microscope. Damp clay feels sticky, but adding water can make it flexible so it can be moulded into different forms and shapes from pots and bricks to ornaments.

ORIGIN Sea bed, freshwater, land

GRAIN SIZE Fine

COLOUR Dark to light grey, white

MINERAL CONTENT
Clay minerals, such as kaolinite, illite, montmorillonite

FOSSILS Plants, invertebrates, vertebrates

Micaceous sandstone

This sandstone contains a high quantity of mica minerals. The mica appears as small flakes in the rock, which are very light and easily blown away in sediments deposited on land. This shows that it's more likely to have been deposited in wate

ORIGIN Sea bed or freshwater

GRAIN SIZE Medium, angular to flattened

COLOUR Buff, green, grey, pink

MINERAL CONTENT Quartz, feldspar, mica

FOSSILS Invertebrates, plants, vertebrates

Septarian nodule

Pale calcite in cracks

The most striking septarian nodules are formed in New Zealand. They formed around 65–55 million years ago.

Nodules and concretions are features that develop after a sedimentary rock forms. Concretions are made of the same minerals as the host rock, but nodules have a different mineral content. Septarian nodules are harder than the surrounding rock. They form when a nodule shrinks and cracks. The cracks fill up with light-coloured minerals such as calcite.

ORIGIN Sea bed, land

GRAIN SIZE Fine to medium, angular to rounded

COLOUR Cream to red

MINERAL CONTENT Calcite or celestine

FOSSILS Vertebrates, invertebrates, plants

The Wave is made of **190** million-year-old sand dunes that have turned to rock

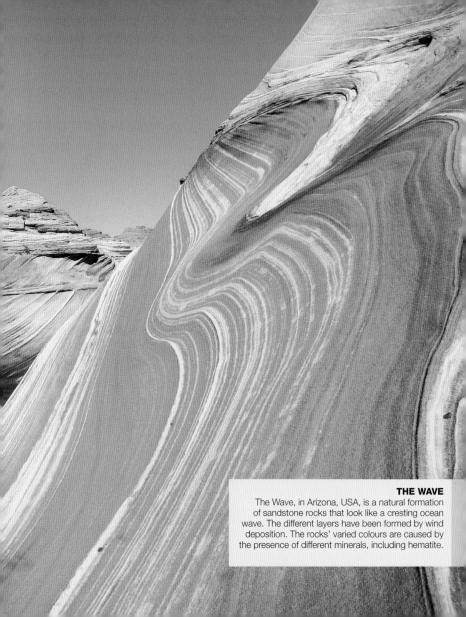

THE WAVE
The Wave, in Arizona, USA, is a natural formation of sandstone rocks that look like a cresting ocean wave. The different layers have been formed by wind deposition. The rocks' varied colours are caused by the presence of different minerals, including hematite.

Metamorphic rocks

When pressure and temperature act upon existing rocks, the atoms and minerals rearrange to form new rocks. These are called metamorphic rocks.

MARBLE

Fine grains and flawless colours make marble ideal for carving.

▲ This marble Arch of Constantine in Rome, Italy, was built in the 4th century CE.

▲ The Taj Mahal in Agra, India, is a huge tomb made of marble.

▲ Michelangelo's statue of David was carved from marble between 1501 and 1504.

Phyllite

Wavy foliation

Phyllite is a dark coloured rock with an irregular surface. The large grains of mica in it make it shiny. It is sometimes used for making pavements.

ORIGINAL ROCK	Mudstone, shale
HOW FORMED	Regional change
TEMPERATURE	Low to moderate
PRESSURE	Low
COLOUR	Silvery to greenish-grey

Marble

Marble fragment

Pure marble is white. Impurities can make it multi-coloured. Some marbles, such as pink and green marble, take their common names from their colour or mineral impurities.

ORIGINAL ROCK   Limestone

HOW FORMED   Regional change, thermal contact

TEMPERATURE   High

PRESSURE   Low to high

COLOUR   White, pink, green, blue, grey

Slate

Slate is an important roofing material and was also used to make chalkboards. It is quarried in large pieces, for use in electrical panels. Plant and animal fossils can be preserved in slate.

ORIGINAL ROCK   Clay, mudstones, shale, tuff

HOW FORMED   Regional change

TEMPERATURE   Low

PRESSURE   Low

COLOUR   Grey, purple, green

Schist

Schist rock has visible mineral grains in it. It is rich in micas or chlorite, and splits easily along crinkly surfaces.

ORIGINAL ROCK   Mud- and clay-based rocks

HOW FORMED   Regional change

TEMPERATURE   Low to moderate

PRESSURE   Low to moderate

COLOUR Silvery, green

Hornfels

This rock forms at temperatures as high as 800°C (1,472°F). There are many varieties depending on the minerals in the rock. Hornfels rock is hard to break.

Hornblende and plagioclase

ORIGINAL ROCK Almost any rock

HOW FORMED Thermal contact

TEMPERATURE Moderate to high

PRESSURE Low to high

COLOUR Dark grey, brown, greenish, reddish

Amphibolite

Roads are often built using amphibolite to give them strength and durability. This rock is also used as an ornamental stone.

ORIGINAL ROCK Basalt greywacke, dolomite

HOW FORMED Regional change

TEMPERATURE Low to moderate

PRESSURE Low to moderate

COLOUR Grey, black, greenish

Quartzite

Quartzite is formed when sandstones are buried, heated, and squeezed. Quartzite is made up of 90 per cent quartz. It is quarried for use as raw material for building roads, laying roofs, and paving blocks.

ORIGINAL ROCK Sandstone
HOW FORMED Regional change
TEMPERATURE High
PRESSURE Low to high
COLOUR White, pink

Fulgurite

The word fulgurite comes from the Latin *fulgur*, meaning "thunderbolt". This rock forms when lightning strikes sand. Lightning in deserts tends to melt the sand, which then fuses into a fulgurite, forming tubes and crusts.

ORIGINAL ROCK Usually sand
HOW FORMED Thermal contact
TEMPERATURE Very high
PRESSURE Low
COLOUR Grey, white, black

Skarn

Skarn is rich in carbonate, calcium, iron, and magnesium silicates. These form different-coloured patches in the rock. Some skarn minerals are rich sources of metals and can be valuable deposits of gold, copper, iron, tin, and zinc.

ORIGINAL ROCK
Limestone, dolomite

HOW FORMED
Thermal contact

TEMPERATURE High

PRESSURE Low

COLOUR Brown

Typical veined and banded structure

Dark mineral bands

Migmatite

Migmatite means "mixed rock". It consists of gneiss or schists mixed with granite. The granite melts slightly, forming streaks that are lighter in colour than the dark bands of gneiss or schists.

ORIGINAL ROCK Various, including granite and gneiss

HOW FORMED Regional change

TEMPERATURE High

PRESSURE High

COLOUR Banded light and dark grey, pink, white

Serpentinite

This rock is the state rock of California, USA. It forms deep within Earth's crust where tectonic plates meet. Made up of serpentine minerals, this rock is known for its marblelike look and feel.

ORIGINAL ROCK Peridotite

HOW FORMED Regional change

TEMPERATURE Low

PRESSURE High

COLOUR Mottled green

Gneiss

This rock is usually found buried deep in mountain-building regions that experience great heat and pressure. As it does not split easily, gneiss is used as a building material for flooring and facing stones. It is also used as an ornamental stone for worktops and even gravestones.

ORIGINAL ROCK	Granite, shale, granodiorite, mudstone, siltstone, or felsic volcanics
HOW FORMED	Regional change
TEMPERATURE	High
PRESSURE	High
COLOUR	Grey, pink, multi-coloured

Mylonite

Mylonite is a crushed rock. It forms on fault planes when movements in Earth's crust exert great pressure but little heat. The pressure exerted on the rock gives it a wavy texture.

ORIGINAL ROCK	Varies
HOW FORMED	Dynamic pressure
TEMPERATURE	Low
PRESSURE	High
COLOUR	Dark or light

Eclogite

Found in the uppermost part of Earth's mantle, eclogite forms at very high temperatures and pressures. It is a coarse-grained rock that is made up of two main minerals – green omphacite pyroxene and red garnet – and often quartz too.

ORIGINAL ROCK	Igneous rocks
HOW FORMED	Regional change
TEMPERATURE	High
PRESSURE	High
COLOUR	Pale green, red

Gneiss is named either from the old German word for spark or the old Saxon word for

decayed
and rotten

BANDED GNEISS

This gneiss rock has been eroded and polished by river water rushing past. This reveals the bands of different minerals that separated and folded into layers as the rock formed. Gneiss forms under very high temperature and pressure.

Meteorites

When parts of rocky asteroids and comets break off in space and fall to Earth, they are called meteorites. As they come from space, they are not classified as igneous, sedimentary, or metamorphic.

FOCUS ON...
CRATERS
When a meteorite lan on Earth, it can caus large impact crater.

Achondrites

Stony meteorites are classified as chondrites and achondrites. The latter are those that do not contain chondrules – miniature igneous rocks that formed in space. Achondrites resemble the rocks found in Earth's mantle and crust.

ORIGIN Space

GRAIN SIZE Medium to coarse

COLOUR Black, grey, yellow

MINERAL CONTENT Pyroxene, olivine, plagioclase feldspar

FOSSILS None

Tektite

When large meteorites hit Earth, they can melt rocks on our planet, which can get thrown in the air and quickly cool to form glass. These glassy objects are called tektites, from the Greek word for "melted".

ORIGIN Meteorite impact

GRAIN SIZE Crystalline

COLOUR Green, black

MINERAL CONTENT Silicate

FOSSILS None

The 168-m- (550-ft-) deep Barringer Meteorite [cr]ater in Arizona, USA, is one of the best known [imp]act craters on Earth.

▲ The circular Lac à l'Eau Claire, or the Clearwater Lakes, in Quebec, Canada, were formed by meteorite impacts around 210 million years ago.

Stony-iron meteorites

[T]hese are mixtures of iron and silicate [m]inerals. Stony-iron meteorites help [s]cientists understand planets such as [M]ars, which has iron and silicate materials.

[O]RIGIN   Space

[G]RAIN SIZE   Fine to medium

[C]OLOUR   Grey, greenish, tan, or black

[M]INERAL CONTENT   Olivine, [p]yroxene, plagioclase

[F]OSSILS   None

Accumulated rock particles

Nickel-iron

Minerals

Minerals are all around us. There are more than 4,500 known minerals, but only 100 of these are common. They are naturally occurring solids that are made up of particular combinations of chemicals. Minerals make up much of our planet and provide many things we use every day, from copper pipes to jewellery to toothpaste.

MALACHITE BOX
This malachite jewel box was made in 1989. Polished malachite is a popular decorative material for buildings and ornaments.

Where minerals form

Minerals form in many different environments – in rocks, in the sea, inside Earth, and even in human bones. The way they grow may be affected by temperature and pressure. Some minerals take thousand of years to develop, while others grow in only a few hours.

Sedimentary minerals

Minerals can form on Earth's surface. When hot, mineral-rich, salty water evaporates, the minerals left behind are known as evaporites. Calcite, which forms limestone rocks, also develops in sea water.

Wulfenite deposits in cracks of lead ore

Mineral veins

Water found in hot springs and beneath volcanoes often carries dissolved minerals. These are deposited in cracks and cavities of rocks, forming mineral veins.

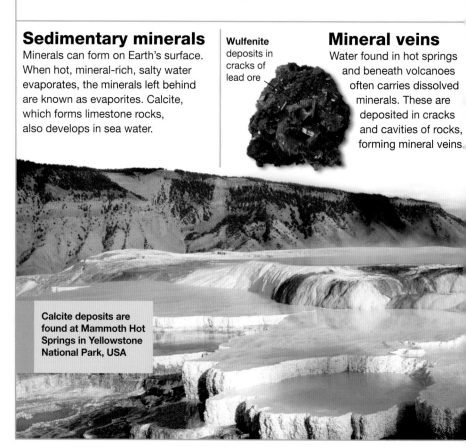

Calcite deposits are found at Mammoth Hot Springs in Yellowstone National Park, USA

Olivine is found in igneous rocks

gneous minerals

agma inside Earth contains chemicals
at are present in minerals. The minerals
velop when magma and lava begin to
ol and solidify to form igneous rocks.

Metamorphic minerals

In mountain-forming areas, heat and
pressure change existing rocks, and new
minerals grow. These metamorphic minerals
usually have a good crystal shape. Some
minerals, such as garnet, form over hundreds
of thousands of years as
heat and pressure
gradually alter
the rocks.

**The mineral
spinel grows when
metamorphic
rocks change**

Mineral groups

There are thousands of minerals on Earth. These have been divided into 12 main groups, or families, based on the chemicals they contain. While some minerals are abundant, others – including diamonds – are very rare and highly prized.

Gold in quartz

Native elements

Most minerals are made from combinations of chemical elements, but a few elements, such as silver, gold, and sulphur, occur naturally by themselves. These are known as native elements.

Sulphides

Sulphur combines with metals to form sulphides. They form near geothermal springs or in veins with quartz. Sulphides include cinnabar and pyrite.

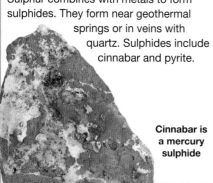

Cinnabar is a mercury sulphide

Sulphosalts

This a group of 200 rare minerals that form when sulphur combines with a metal (silver, copper, lead, or iron) and a semi-metal (arsenic or antimony).

Proustite contains arsenic

Oxides

Oxides form when oxygen combines with metals. They include ores (minerals from which metals are extracted) and gems.

Rutile forms when titanium and oxygen combine

Hydroxides

These minerals form when a metallic element combines with hydrogen and oxygen. These minerals are less dense than oxides and tend to be softer. Hydroxides are also important ore minerals. They include bauxite, which is an ore of aluminium.

Bauxite

Halides

In these soft minerals, metals combine with chlorine, bromine, fluorine, or iodine. For example, sylvite is a combination of potassium and chlorine.

Glassy, cube-shaped **crystals**

Sylvite

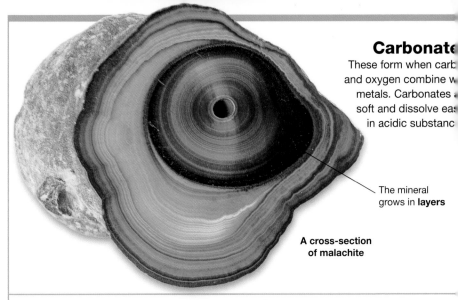

Carbonate[s]

These form when carb[on] and oxygen combine w[ith] metals. Carbonates [are] soft and dissolve ea[sily] in acidic substanc[es].

The mineral grows in **layers**

A cross-section of malachite

Erythrite is an arsenate

Phosphates, arsenates, and vanadates

These rare minerals are grouped together because they have a similar structure, made up of oxygen combined with phosphorus, arsenic, or vanadium. They often have vivid colours.

Borates and nitrates

Borates form when a metallic element combines with boron and oxygen. Wh[en] nitrogen and oxygen combine with a metallic element, nitrates are formed.

Glassy lustre

Boracite crystals

alcanthite
sulphate

Sulphates, chromates, molybdates, tungstates

Around 200 minerals make up this large group. They share a similar structure and elements – oxygen combined with a metal or semi-metal. These minerals are dense, brittle, and may be vividly coloured.

Silicates

This group makes up a quarter of all known minerals. As well as being common, silicates such as feldspar and quartz are important rock-forming minerals. Other silicates include mica, garnet, and natrolite. All silicates contain silicon and oxygen.

Natrolite

Organic minerals

These are a group of minerals that form from living things, and may or may not have a crystal structure. Amber, coral, and pearl are organic gems. Amber forms from the resin of conifer trees, coral from sea creatures, and pearl comes from certain shellfish and oysters.

Red coral

Identifying minerals

There are many ways to identify a mineral, including observing its colour and shape, and how it looks when light reflects off it. The hardness of a mineral can be measured by how easily it scratches.

Crystal systems

Minerals have different "crystal systems", or crystal shapes. There are six groups:

Cubic

Monoclinic

Triclinic

Trigonal/ hexagonal

Orthorhombic

Tetragona

Cleavage

Cleavage describes how easily and cleanly a mineral breaks along its natural weak points. Perfect cleavage produces a smooth, shiny surface. Cleavage can also be difficult, distinct, or "none" (leaving rough, uneven surfaces).

Obsidian
fractures wi
a conchoida
or shell-like
pattern

Iceland spar, a type of calcite, cleaves to make a perfect rhombic shape

Fracture

This is how cleanly a mineral breaks in places other than its cleavage lines. Fractu can leave jagged edges (hackly), rough but flat surfaces (even), shell-like scoops (conchoidal), or no pattern at all (uneven).

Habit

A mineral's habit, or general shape, depends on the pattern that its crystals form as they grow. If there is no clear shape, it is called "massive".

Scolecite looks like needles

Copper has a plantlike shape

Actinolite looks like knife blades

Beryl looks like a prism with a regular shape

Finger
nail: 2.5

Hardness

Mohs' scale, invented by the mineralogist Friedrich Mohs, measures how hard a mineral is based on how easily it scratches. The scale consists of 10 minerals arranged from 1 to 10. The higher the number, the harder the mineral. Every mineral can scratch the ones listed below it and get scratched by minerals above it on the scale.

MOHS' SCALE OF HARDNESS

1: Talc	2: Gypsum	3: Calcite	4: Fluorite	5: Apatite
6: Orthoclase	7: Quartz	8: Topaz	9: Corundum	10: Diamond

Specific gravity (SG)

This is a measure of how heavy a mineral is compared to an equal volume of water.

The SG of jasper is 2.7, meaning it is 2.7 times heavier than water.

Colour

Some minerals come in more than one colour. Usually this is because the mineral contains impurities or its crystals are flawed.

Fluorite is known for its many different colours.

Streak

When a mineral is crushed into a powder and drawn on porcelain, it produces a streak. The colour of the streak may not be the same as the mineral colour.

Orpiment

Cinnabar

Crocoite

Chalcopyrite

Hematite

Molybdenite

Transparency

If light can pass through a mineral, it is called translucent. If a mineral is opaque, no light can pass through it. Transparent minerals are clear and see-through.

Transparent

Translucent

Opaque

Lustre

This describes how shiny a mineral is when sunlight reflects off it. Lustres include dull, greasy, silky, metallic, waxy, and vitreous (glassy). The shiniest is adamantine (diamondlike).

Galena looks like metal when light reflects off it

Quartz has a glasslike, or vitreous, lustre

Metallic

Vitreous

Gemstones

Some minerals are brilliantly coloured and form striking and large crystals that are used as gemstones. They are valued for their beauty and rarity – there's nothing chemical that makes gemstones different from other minerals. More than 4,500 minerals exist, but only 100 are used as gemstones.

Gemstones often look **dull** before they are cut and polished

Uncut Burmese ruby crystal

Cutting and polishing

To bring out the beauty of gemstones, they are cut and polished. Coloured stones, such as rubies, are cut in different ways to bring out the rich colours. Opaque or translucent stones are generally cut into a smooth oval. Some gems may be beautiful but too soft or brittle to be cut and worn.

Different cuts bring out the beauty of a gemstone

Mixed cut ruby

Brilliant cut aquamarine

Step cut zircon

Precious gems

There are two kinds of gem: precious and semi-precious. Only seven gemstones – diamond, aquamarine, emerald, sapphire, ruby, topaz, and opal – are regarded as precious. Jewellers use different gemstone cuts, colours, and combinations to make dazzling pieces of jewellery.

Emerald

Ruby

Sapphire

Koh-i-Noor is a part of the British Crown Jewels

rganic gems

ost gems come from rocks, but some have organic origin, which means they come from ing things. For example, pearls form in certain ellfish and oysters. Others clude coral (from a creatures), nber (from ee resin), and t (from coal).

Pearl on oyster shell

Megagems

Some gemstones stand out for their extraordinary beauty and size. These are called megagems. The Koh-i-Noor diamond weighs 109 carats (21.8 g/0.77 oz).

Native elements

Chemical elements that occur in nature by themselves rather than with other elements are called native elements. They can be classified into three groups: metals, semi-metals, and non-metals.

▲ Worldwide, dentists use about 23 kg (50 lb) of gold a day for making tooth fillings.

▲ Many microchips in computers are made of gold circuits that allow data to flow in the computer.

▲ The plastic visor of an astronaut's spacesuit helmet is coated with gold to protect the astronaut from the Sun's glare.

Copper

Native copper is found close to Earth's surface above other copper deposits. Copper in its natural state was probably the first metal used by people, who made it into weapons and tools as a substitute for stone. It is now used in electrical wires and deep-sea cables, among other things.

HARDNESS 2.5–3	**SG** 8.9
COLOUR Copper-red to brown	
TRANSPARENCY Opaque	
LUSTRE Metallic	

Platinum

Platinum is rarer than gold. As well as being used in jewellery, it is also used to refine fuel to reduce pollution from cars.

HARDNESS 4–4.5	SG 14–19
COLOUR Whitish steel-grey	
TRANSPARENCY Opaque	
LUSTRE Metallic	

Gold

Gold has been a measure of wealth since ancient times. It is ideal for making jewellery because it is soft and can be easily worked into different shapes. Jewellers sometimes mix it with metals such as silver and copper to make it harder. Gold is also valued because it does not lose its colour or lustre when exposed to air. South Africa is the largest producer of gold in the world.

HARDNESS 2.5–3	SG 19.3
COLOUR Golden-yellow	
TRANSPARENCY Opaque	
LUSTRE Metallic	

Silver

A strong conductor of electricity and heat, silver is widely used in the electrical industry. It is a popular raw material in the making of jewellery and coins. The leading producer of silver is Peru.

HARDNESS 2.5–3	SG 10.1–11.1
COLOUR Silver-white	
TRANSPARENCY Opaque	
LUSTRE Metallic	

Sulphur

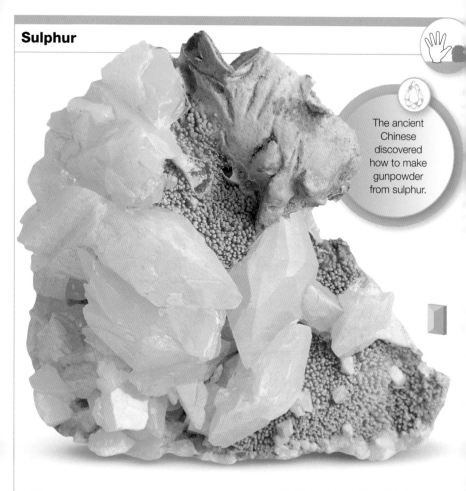

The ancient Chinese discovered how to make gunpowder from sulphur.

Sulphur forms around hot springs and volcanic craters. It burns with a blue flame if held over a lighted match. Mined on a large scale, sulphur is widely used in explosives, fertilizers, dyes, drugs, and detergents.

HARDNESS	1.5–2.5
SG	2.1
COLOUR	Yellow
TRANSPARENCY	Transparent to translucent
LUSTRE	Resinous to greasy

Diamond

A pure form of carbon, diamond is the hardest mineral on Earth. Diamond-tipped drills and saws can cut through any substance. The glittery brilliance of diamond makes it the most valuable gemstone in the world.

HARDNESS 10   **SG** 3.4–3.5

COLOUR White to black, colourless, yellow, pink, red, blue, brown

TRANSPARENCY Transparent to opaque

LUSTRE Diamondlike

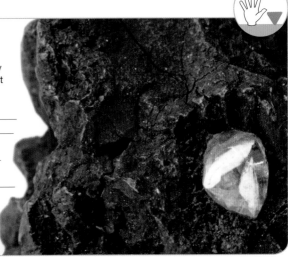

Graphite

This mineral takes its name from the Greek word *graphein*, which means "to write". It leaves a black mark when rubbed on paper and is used in pencils. It is also one of the softest minerals and can be cut with a knife.

HARDNESS 1–2

SG 2.2

COLOUR Black

TRANSPARENCY Opaque

LUSTRE Metallic or dull earthy

Iron

Iron makes up 5 per cent of Earth's crust. After oxygen, silicon, and aluminium, it is the fourth most abundant chemical in the crust. It is used to make a vast number of things, including steel, magnets, and car parts.

HARDNESS 4.5   **SG** 7.3–7.9

COLOUR Steel-grey to iron-black

TRANSPARENCY Opaque

LUSTRE Metallic

Nickel-iron

Often found in meteorites on Earth's surface, nickel-iron used to be called "sky-iron" by the ancient Egyptians. They used it to make sacred tools for mummifying pharaohs.

HARDNESS 4-5		**SG** 7.3–8.2	

COLOUR Steel-grey, dark grey, blackish

TRANSPARENCY Opaque

LUSTRE Metallic

Bismuth

This rare native element is mostly found in hydrothermal veins and pegmatites. It is a semi-metal – it expands on freezing, just as water expands when it turns into ice.

HARDNESS 2–2.5

SG 9.7–9.8

COLOUR Silver-white with reddish tarnish

TRANSPARENCY Opaque

LUSTRE Metallic

Arsenic

When heated, this mineral quickly turns into gas without melting. Though poisonous, it was used in some medicines to treat infections. Arsenic was also used to make pesticides.

HARDNESS 3.5

SG 5.7

COLOUR Tin-white

TRANSPARENCY Opaque

LUSTRE Metallic or dull earthy

Mercury

Native mercury exists in a poisonous, liquid form at room temperature. It is used in thermometers because even a minor change in temperature can cause it to expand or contract.

HARDNESS Liquid	SG 13.6–14.4
COLOUR Silver-white	
TRANSPARENCY Opaque	
LUSTRE Metallic	

Mercury was named after the Roman god of trade.

The **deepest** point in the Danakil desert is 100 m (328 ft) below sea level

SULPHUR
Earth's lowest lying desert, the Danakil in Ethiopia, is known for its extreme heat. It is made up of volcanoes, hot springs, and acidic ponds. Bright yellow sulphur crystallizes around volcanic craters, adding beautiful shapes and colour to the landscape.

Sulphides

In these minerals, sulphur combines with one or more metals. They have a metallic lustre and can conduct electricity, but not as well as metals. They are important sources of lead, zinc, iron, and copper and a good source of silver and platinum.

▲ The blue colour in fireworks comes from stibnite, which is a source of antimony.

▲ Roman ingots are made of lead, which is extracted from galena and other lead sulphides.

◀ Cinnabar contains mercury, which is used in thermometers.

Galena

A valuable mineral since Roman times, galena is the principle ore of lead. It develops mineral-rich cubic crystals, which form when hot fluids find their way to higher levels in Earth's crust.

HARDNESS	2.5
SG	7.6
COLOUR	Lead-grey
TRANSPARENCY	Opaque
LUSTRE	Metallic

phalerite

phalerite can occur in several different
rms and is often mistaken for galena.
is sulphide is an important source of zinc
d can also be used as a gemstone.

ARDNESS 3–4

G 3.9–4.1

OLOUR Brown, black, yellow

RANSPARENCY Opaque
transparent

USTRE Resinous to
amondlike, metallic

---

canthite

ccurring as spiky crystals, acanthite
kes its name from the Greek word *akantha*,
eaning "thorn". This sulphide is the main
urce of silver.

ARDNESS 2–2.5   **SG** 7.2–7.4

OLOUR Black

RANSPARENCY Opaque

USTRE Metallic

Bornite

Known as "peacock ore" because of its
iridescent splash of colours, bornite is a
source of copper. Bornite crystals are rarely
found as it usually occurs as massive aggregates.

HARDNESS 3	**SG** 5.1

COLOUR Coppery red, brown

TRANSPARENCY
Opaque

LUSTRE
Metallic

Covellite

This sulphide of copper is named after the Italian Nicolas Covelli, who first described it. It was first collected and identified at Mount Vesuvius, near Naples, Italy. When heated, covellite produces a blue-coloured flame.

HARDNESS	1.5–2
SG	4.6–4.7
COLOUR	Indigo-blue to black
TRANSPARENCY	Opaque
LUSTRE	Submetallic to resinous

Pentlandite

Named after Irish scientist Joseph Pentland, pentlandite is a major ore of nickel. Nickel ores need extensive refining for releasing the metal. Deposits have been found in Canada and Russia, and also in meteorites.

HARDNESS	3.5–4
SG	4.6–5
COLOUR	Bronze-yellow
TRANSPARENCY	Opaque
LUSTRE	Metallic

Cinnabar

Highly poisonous, cinnabar is the main ore of mercury. It is the central ingredient in the pigment vermilion, and its brilliant orange-red colour was used in paintings in ancient China. Cinnabar often forms around volcanic vents and hot springs.

HARDNESS	2–2.5	**SG**	8
COLOUR	Red		
TRANSPARENCY	Transparent to opaque		
LUSTRE	Diamondlike to dull		

Greenockite

This mineral is a cadmium ore, which is used for plating steel and other metals that get corroded easily. It is mixed with nickel to make rechargeable batteries.

HARDNESS 3–3.5   **SG** 4.8–4.9

COLOUR Yellow, orange, orange-yellow, red

TRANSPARENCY Nearly opaque to translucent

LUSTRE Resinous or diamondlike

Greenockite coating

Pyrrhotite

This magnetic mineral is a mixture of iron and sulphur in varying amounts. The amount of iron affects its magnetic properties. The mineral name is derived from the Greek word *pyrrhos*, which means "flame-coloured".

HARDNESS 3.5–4.5   **SG** 4.6–4.7

COLOUR Bronze-yellow to copper bronze-red

TRANSPARENCY Opaque

LUSTRE Metallic

Realgar

After handling realgar, it's important to wash your hands because of the arsenic content.

Characterized by its bright red crystals, realgar has been used in Chinese art and for making fireworks. However, when exposed to light, the crystals crumble and form a yellow crust. Realgar is an important ore of the poison arsenic and is itself poisonous.

HARDNESS 1.5–2	SG 3.6
COLOUR Scarlet to orange-yellow	
TRANSPARENCY Subtransparent to opaque	
LUSTRE Resinous to greasy	

Chalcocite

One of the most important ores of copper, chalcocite crystals were mined in Cornwall, England, for centuries. Copper is used for making aircraft, and other commercial and domestic purposes.

HARDNESS	2.5–3
SG	5.5–5.8
COLOUR	Blackish lead-grey
TRANSPARENCY	Opaque
LUSTRE	Metallic

Stannite

Stannite, an ore of tin, is found at Zeehan in Tasmania, Australia, and Cornwall in England. It occurs in tin-bearing, hydrothermal veins and rarely forms crystals.

HARDNESS	4	**SG**	4.4
COLOUR	Steel-grey to iron-black		
TRANSPARENCY	Opaque		
LUSTRE	Metallic		

Chalcopyrite

Though not very rich in copper, its widespread occurrence makes chalcopyrite an important copper ore. It is commonly found in hydrothermal ore veins deposited at high and medium temperatures.

HARDNESS	3.5–4
SG	4.2
COLOUR	Brass-yellow
TRANSPARENCY	Opaque
LUSTRE	Metallic

Stibnite

Stibnite's long, prism-shaped crystals have an unusual property – they can grow twisted and bent. Stibnite is the main ore of antimony, which is used for hardening lead and is added to paint and plastics as a flame-retardant.

HARDNESS 2		**SG** 4.6	
COLOUR Lead-grey to steel-grey, black			
TRANSPARENCY Opaque			
LUSTRE Metallic			

Prismlike crystals

In ancient times, powdered stibnite was used as make-up to darken eyelashes and eyebrows.

Millerite

This sulphide is an ore of nickel, used in metal alloys. It forms in needle-like crystals or in masses. It normally forms at low temperatures in holes in limestone or dolomite rocks, and is also found in meteorites. Millerite is named after English mineralogist W H Miller who first studied it.

Calcite groundmass

Millerite crystal

HARDNESS	3–3.5
SG	5.5
COLOUR	Brass-yellow
TRANSPARENCY	Opaque
LUSTRE	Metallic

Orpiment

Orpiment takes its name from the Latin *auri pigmentum*, meaning "golden paint". Pigment derived from it was used in 19th-century paintings. However, it contains arsenic, which is poisonous.

HARDNESS 1.5–2	**SG** 3.5
COLOUR Yellow	
TRANSPARENCY Transparent to translucent	
LUSTRE Resinous	

Pyrite

Bismuthinite

This rare mineral is a source of bismuth. When bismuth is mixed with other metals, it has a low melting point and is used in fire-safety devices, such as sprinkler heads.

HARDNESS 2
SG 6.8
COLOUR Lead-grey to tin-white
TRANSPARENCY Opaque
LUSTRE Metallic

Marcasite

In the late Victorian era, marcasite was used to make mourning jewellery, worn at funeral ceremonies and other sombre occasions. Its crystals tend to darken with exposure to air.

HARDNESS 6–6.5
SG 4.9
COLOUR Pale bronze-yellow
TRANSPARENCY Opaque
LUSTRE Metallic

Chalk groundmass

Also called fool's gold, pyrite was often mistaken for gold because of its brassy colour and high density. Pyrite gets its name from Greek *pyr*, meaning "fire", as it emits sparks when struck by iron.

Cubic habit

HARDNESS	6–6.5
SG	5
COLOUR	Pale brass-yellow
TRANSPARENCY	Opaque
LUSTRE	Metallic

Hauerite

This manganese sulphide occurs in areas with salt deposits. It is found in Texas, USA; the Ural Mountains of Russia; and Sicily, Italy.

HARDNESS	4
SG	3.5
COLOUR	Red-brown to brown-black
TRANSPARENCY	Opaque
LUSTRE	Diamondlike to submetallic

Cobaltite

Also known as cobalt glance, cobaltite is a source of cobalt. Cobalt is mixed with metals to make machine parts stronger and heat-resistant.

HARDNESS	5.5
SG	6.3
COLOUR	Silver-white, pink
TRANSPARENCY	Opaque
LUSTRE	Metallic

Arsenopyrite

This mineral is found in metamorphic and igneous rocks, in ore veins that form at moderate to high temperatures. It is the main source of arsenic and the most common of the minerals that contain this poison.

HARDNESS 5.5–6	**SG** 6.1
COLOUR Silver-white to steel-grey	
TRANSPARENCY Opaque	
LUSTRE Metallic	

Crystals are marked with grooves

When heated or struck, arsenopyrite gives off an odour that smells like garlic.

Molybdenite

This sulphide was originally mistaken for lead and so its name came from the Greek word for lead, *molybdos*. When added to alloys, it increases the hardness of iron and steel, protecting them against corrosion.

HARDNESS 1–1.5	**SG** 4.7
COLOUR Lead-grey	
TRANSPARENCY Opaque	
LUSTRE Metallic	

Sylvanite

Sylvanite is often found in small quantities in gold and silver deposits. It is photosensitive, which means it reacts to light, and can acquire a dark tarnish if exposed to bright light for too long.

HARDNESS 1–2	**SG** 8.2
COLOUR Silver-white to pale yellow	
TRANSPARENCY Opaque	
LUSTRE Metallic	

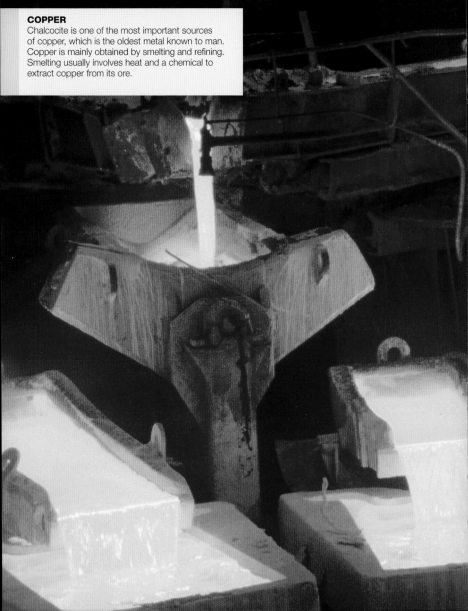

COPPER

Chalcocite is one of the most important sources of copper, which is the oldest metal known to man. Copper is mainly obtained by smelting and refining. Smelting usually involves heat and a chemical to extract copper from its ore.

Copper was the first metal to be separated from its ore, probably around **10,000 years ago**

Sulphosalts

Sulphosalts are a large group of mostly rare minerals in which sulphur combines with a metal and a non-metal. They have a lustre similar to that of a metal and are dense and brittle.

FOCUS ON...
SITES

There are several sites across the world that are known for their sources of sulphosalts.

▲ The Giant Mountains in Czech Republic are a key site for polybasite and proustite.

▲ Jamesonite and atennantite are found in abundance in Chihuahua, Mexico.

▲ The Harz Mountains in Germany are a source of many sulphosalts, such as bournonite, boulangerite, and zinkenite.

Tetrahedrite

Tetrahedrite is an important ore of copper and has been mined all over the world for centuries. It is also sometimes mined for its silver content. Austria, Germany, England, Mexico, and Peru are some of the important sites for tetrahedrite.

HARDNESS	3–4
SG	4.6–5.1
COLOUR	Flint-grey to iron-black
TRANSPARENCY	Opaque
LUSTRE	Metallic

Pyrargyrite

Pyrargyrite is
an important
source of silver.
Also called dark
ruby silver, it
darkens when
exposed to
light. Its name
derives from the
Greek words *pyr,* meaning
"fire", and *argent*, meaning "silver".

HARDNESS 2.5	SG 5.8
COLOUR Deep red	
TRANSPARENCY Translucent	
LUSTRE Diamondlike	

Proustite

Proustite is sensitive to light and turns
from transparent scarlet to opaque grey
when exposed to strong light. Its bright
wine-red crystals make attractive gems. Chile
and Germany are notable sources of this mineral.

HARDNESS 2–2.5
SG 5.8
COLOUR Scarlet, grey
TRANSPARENCY Translucent
LUSTRE Diamondlike to submetallic

Bournonite

A combination of copper, lead,
antimony, and sulphur, bournonite forms
tablet-shaped prismatic crystals. Some of
the crystals found in the mineral-rich Harz
Mountains of Germany have a diameter
of 2.5 cm (1 in) or more. It has been
nicknamed "cogwheel ore" as it
sometimes develops crystals in
the shape of a cogwheel.

HARDNESS 2.5–3
SG 5.8
COLOUR Steel-grey
TRANSPARENCY Opaque
LUSTRE Metallic

Oxides

These minerals form when oxygen combines with a metal or semi-metal. In simple oxides, only a single metal or semi-metal is present, but multiple oxides may contain several.

FOCUS ON...
MAJOR ORE:
Some minerals are mined as ores as the contain useful eleme such as metals.

Ruby

Known in Sanskrit as *ratnaraj* or "king of precious stones", ruby is the red variety of corundum, the hardest mineral on Earth after diamond. Heating improves its colour and clarity. Crystals of ruby tend to be small, as the presence of chromium hampers their growth. Therefore, large rubies have high value. Several myths and beliefs are associated with ruby. In Burmese tradition, ruby bestows good fortune and invincibility, and Russians traditionally consider it to be good for the heart, brain, blood purification, and vitality.

HARDNESS 9	**SG** 4–4.1

COLOUR Red

TRANSPARENCY
Transparent to translucent

LUSTRE Diamondlike to glassy

The mineral cuprite is an ore copper – which is widely used making electrical wires.

▲ Chromite is a significant source of the metal chromium. It is mixed with steel when manufacturing stainless steel.

▲ Titanium, which comes from rutile, is very strong and is used in aircraft, spacecraft, missiles, and ships.

Sapphire

Another variety of corundum is sapphire. It is most abundant in metamorphic rocks, and large deposits are quite rare. This oxide is "pleochroic", which means it appears in different colours when viewed from different angles. Despite their hardness, sapphires are also carved or engraved. The 423-carat Logan Sapphire, mined in Sri Lanka, is believed to be the world's largest blue sapphire.

HARDNESS	9	SG	4–4.1

COLOUR Occurs in most colours

TRANSPARENCY Transparent to translucent

LUSTRE Diamondlike to glassy

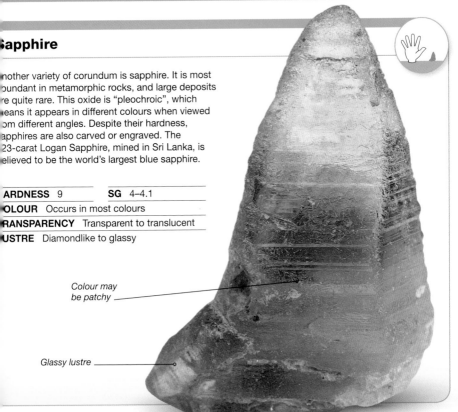

Colour may be patchy

Glassy lustre

Magnetite

This mineral is so highly magnetic, it will attract iron and can move a compass needle. The ancient Chinese made their first compasses with magnetite.

HARDNESS 5.5–6	SG 5.2

COLOUR Black to brownish-black

TRANSPARENCY Opaque

LUSTRE Metallic to semi-metallic

Spinel

The red variety of this mineral is hard and is cut as a gemstone. It looks similar to ruby – the Black Prince's Ruby in the British Imperial State Crown was found to be a spinel.

HARDNESS 7.5–8	SG 3.6

COLOUR Red, yellow, orange-red, blue, green, brown, black

TRANSPARENCY Transparent to translucent

LUSTRE Glassy

Cassiterite

A tin oxide, cassiterite derives its name from *kassiteros*, the Greek word for "tin". It is a major source of tin and is found in China, Malaysia, and Indonesia.

HARDNESS 6–7	SG 7

COLOUR Medium to dark brown

TRANSPARENCY Transparent to opaque

LUSTRE Diamondlike to metallic

Zincite

Also known as red oxide of zinc, zincite rarely forms crystals. It is found in Sterling Hill, New Jersey, USA.

Zincite

HARDNESS 4

SG 5.7

COLOUR Orange-yellow to deep red

TRANSPARENCY Almost opaque

LUSTRE Resinous

Chromite

Chromite is the major source of chromium. This metal is mixed with iron to make high-speed tools and stainless steel.

HARDNESS 5.5		**SG** 4.7
COLOUR Dark brown, black		
TRANSPARENCY Opaque		
LUSTRE Metallic		

Chrysoberyl

This mineral has been used in Asia for thousands of years as an amulet to protect against "the evil eye". Its gemstone variety, alexandrite, is one of the rarest and most expensive gems.

HARDNESS 8.5
SG 3.7
COLOUR Green, yellow
TRANSPARENCY Transparent to translucent
LUSTRE Glassy

Hematite

Hematite is the most important ore of iron. Its name is derived from the Greek *aimatitis*, meaning "blood-red" – a reference to the red colour of its powder. It has long been associated with blood – bones of Neolithic burials have been found smeared with hematite powder.

HARDNESS 5–6		**SG** 5.3
COLOUR Steel-grey		
TRANSPARENCY Opaque		
LUSTRE Metallic to dull		

Perovskite

Found in Earth's upper mantle, Perovskite was first discovered in the Ural Mountains of Russia.

HARDNESS 5.5
SG 4
COLOUR Black, brown, yellow
TRANSPARENCY Transparent to opaque
LUSTRE Diamondlike, metallic

Uraninite

A radioactive mineral, uraninite is the main source of uranium, which is used to power nuclear reactors. In earlier times, it was used in small amounts for colouring ceramics.

HARDNESS 5–6	SG 6.5–11

COLOUR Black to brownish-black, dark grey, greenish

TRANSPARENCY Opaque

LUSTRE Submetallic, pitchy, dull

Samarskite

Named after Russian mining engineer Vasili Samarski-Bykhovets, samarskite contains uranium and has radioactive crystals. It was discovered in Miass, Russia.

HARDNESS 5–6	SG 5.7

COLOUR Black

TRANSPARENCY Translucent to opaque

LUSTRE Glassy to resinous

Brookite

This mineral is named after English crystallographer H J Brooke. It is one of the few naturally occurring polymorphs (a mineral that can crystallize in different forms).

HARDNESS 5.5–6	SG 4.1

COLOUR Various shades of brown

TRANSPARENCY Opaque to transparent

LUSTRE Metallic to diamondlike

Brookite

Pyrochlore

This mineral gets its name from Greek words for "fire" and "green" because it turns green after heating. It is an important source of niobium, a soft grey metal used mostly in alloys such as steel.

HARDNESS	5–5.5
SG	4.5
COLOUR	Brown to black
TRANSPARENCY	Translucent to opaque
LUSTRE	Glassy to resinous

Albite

Rutile

Rutile takes its name from Latin word *rutilis*, meaning "red" or "glowing". Rutile can grow inside quartz, where it is pale golden rather than dark yellowish or reddish brown. Rutilated quartz has been used as an ornamental stone since ancient times.

Vertical grooves

HARDNESS	6–6.5	SG	4.2
COLOUR	Reddish-brown to red		
TRANSPARENCY	Transparent to opaque		
LUSTRE	Diamondlike to submetallic		

Hydroxides

Hydroxides form when a metal combines with water and oxygen at a low temperature. They are usually found in sedimentary rocks and are often important ore minerals. Many hydroxide minerals are very soft.

Diaspore

Diaspore takes its name from the Greek word for "scatter", because when it is heated, it crackles and scatters light. This makes it look as though it has different colours when seen from different angles.

HARDNESS 6.5–7	**SG** 3.4	
COLOUR White, grey, yellow, lilac, or pink		
TRANSPARENCY Transparent to translucent		
LUSTRE Glassy		

Bauxite

Bauxite is a mixture of several minerals that include aluminium oxides or hydroxides. Technically it is a rock, but it's usually grouped with minerals. It is an important source of aluminium. Of all the bauxite mined, 90 per cent is used to extract aluminium.

HARDNESS 1–3	**SG** 2.3–2.7	
COLOUR White, yellowish, red, reddish-brown		
TRANSPARENCY Opaque		
LUSTRE Earthy		

Goethite

German poet and author Johann Wolfgang von Goethe was an enthusiastic mineralogist, and goethite is named after him. It is an iron oxide hydroxide and can occur as grooved crystals.

HARDNESS 5–5.5

SG 4.3

COLOUR Orangish to blackish-brown

TRANSPARENCY Translucent to opaque

LUSTRE Diamondlike to metallic

Limonite

Limonite has been used as a pigment in painting since ancient Egyptian times, and was also used by the Dutch portrait artist Anthony van Dyck. It forms as a secondary mineral when other minerals oxidize (react with oxygen), and doesn't form crystals.

HARDNESS 4–5.5

SG 2.7–4.3

COLOUR Various shades of brown, yellow

TRANSPARENCY Opaque

LUSTRE Earthy, sometimes submetallic or dull

Halides

Halides are soft minerals and have a low specific gravity. These minerals form when metals combine with one of the common halogen elements, which include fluorine, chlorine, bromine, and iodine.

FOCUS ON...
USES AT HOME

Many halides can be found in our homes and are used on a daily basis.

▲ Cryolite is used in the production of aluminium, which gives us aluminium foil.

▲ Halite, or common salt, is used as a preservative and as seasoning in foods.

▲ Fluorine, from fluorite, is used to give cooking pans a non-stick surface.

Halite

Halite is common edible salt, or sodium chloride. A vital mineral for human and animal health, salt is also used as a preservative and in making soap and glass. Halite forms as salty deposits when saltwater evaporates, and is found worldwide.

HARDNESS	2.5	SG	2.1–2.6
COLOUR	Colourless to white		
TRANSPARENCY	Transparent to translucent		
LUSTRE	Glassy		

Fluorite

Fluorite melts easily, and its name comes from the Latin *fluere*, "to flow". When seen under ultraviolet light, this mineral is fluorescent (it gives off a glowing light).

HARDNESS 4	SG 3.2–3.6

COLOUR Occurs in most colours

TRANSPARENCY Transparent to translucent

LUSTRE Glassy

Cryolite

Molten cryolite was mixed with aluminium oxides for the manufacture of aircraft and engineering products.

HARDNESS 2.5	SG 3

COLOUR Colourless to snow-white

TRANSPARENCY Transparent to translucent

LUSTRE Glassy to greasy

Carnallite

Carnallite forms when potassium and magnesium chloride mix with water. It is an important source of the chemical potash.

HARDNESS 2.5	SG 1.6

COLOUR Milky white, often reddish

TRANSPARENCY Translucent to opaque

LUSTRE Greasy

Atacamite

The Statue of Liberty in New York, USA, is coloured green by a layer of atacamite. It is named after the Atacama Desert in Chile.

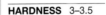

HARDNESS 3–3.5	SG 3.8

COLOUR Bright green to blackish-green

TRANSPARENCY Transparent to translucent

LUSTRE Diamondlike to glassy

The world's largest salt flat, Salar de Uyuni contains around

10 billion

tonnes of salt

HALITE
Large crystals of halite, or common salt, forms after the evaporation of water from the sea or saltwater lakes. Salar de Uyuni, in Bolivia, is the remains of a prehistoric salt lake. It covers an area of 10,582 sq km (4,086 sq miles).

Carbonates

Carbonate minerals form when a carbonate (carbon and oxygen) combines with metals or semi-metals. They can be found in sea shells, coral reefs, and rocks such as marble and chalk.

FOCUS ON...
CALCITE
Most carbonates fou
in Earth's crust are
calcite – a useful forn
of calcium carbonate

Smithsonite

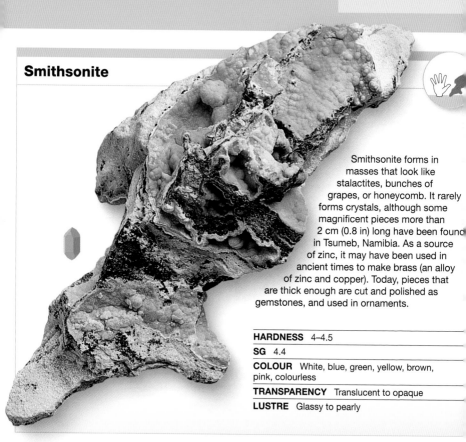

Smithsonite forms in masses that look like stalactites, bunches of grapes, or honeycomb. It rarely forms crystals, although some magnificent pieces more than 2 cm (0.8 in) long have been found in Tsumeb, Namibia. As a source of zinc, it may have been used in ancient times to make brass (an alloy of zinc and copper). Today, pieces that are thick enough are cut and polished as gemstones, and used in ornaments.

HARDNESS	4–4.5
SG	4.4
COLOUR	White, blue, green, yellow, brown, pink, colourless
TRANSPARENCY	Translucent to opaque
LUSTRE	Glassy to pearly

White and yellow
calcite was quarried in
ancient Egypt and used
in buildings and statues.

▲ Marble is another
form of calcite. Strong
and decorative, it is still
used in buildings today.

▲ Found inside caves,
calcite forms long, thin
stalactites that build up
as water drips.

▲ Calcium carbonate
taken from calcite is
the main ingredient for
indigestion tablets.

Calcite

One of the three most common
carbonates on Earth, this calcium
carbonate grows anywhere that water can reach.
Shellfish make their shells from calcite, which
they take from sea water. Calcite is known for its
beautiful crystals, and although it can be almost
any colour, in its pure form it is white or colourless.

HARDNESS 3

SG 2.7

COLOUR Colourless,
white, yellow, black, green

TRANSPARENCY
Transparent to
translucent

LUSTRE
Glassy

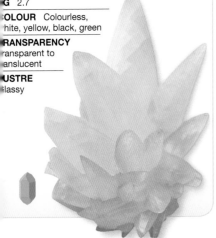

Siderite

This shiny mineral is an iron
carbonate and takes its
name from the Greek
sideros, meaning
"iron". Its crystals
often have curved
faces. When
heated, siderite
becomes
magnetic.

HARDNESS 3.5–4	**SG** 3.9
COLOUR Yellowish-brown to dark brown	
TRANSPARENCY Translucent	
LUSTRE Glassy to pearly	

Aragonite

Formed at low temperatures near Earth's surface, aragonite is found in caves and around hot springs. It forms different shapes, including one that resembles coral. In this shape it is called *flos-ferri*, meaning "flowers of iron".

HARDNESS	3.5–4
SG	2.9
COLOUR	Colourless, white, grey, yellowish, reddish, green
TRANSPARENCY	Transparent to translucent
LUSTRE	Glassy inclining to resinous

Malachite

Malachite is possibly one of the oldest known sources of copper. In ancient Egypt, it was used as an eye paint, probably to prevent eye infections.

HARDNESS	3.5–4	SG	3.9–4
COLOUR	Bright green		
TRANSPARENCY	Translucent		
LUSTRE	Diamondlike to silky		

Rhodochrosite

Gem-quality crystals of this manganese carbonate can be found in the USA and South Africa. These are sometimes cut for collectors. The more common form has a band of colours and is used as decorative stone.

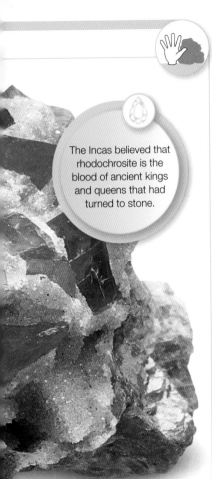

The Incas believed that rhodochrosite is the blood of ancient kings and queens that had turned to stone.

Aurichalcite

Aurichalcite is Latin for "golden copper". It has a distinctive velvetlike coating. It burns with a green flame because it contains copper.

HARDNESS 1–2	SG 4.2
COLOUR Sky-blue, green-blue, or pale green	
TRANSPARENCY Transparent to translucent	
LUSTRE Silky to pearly	

Ankerite

Harder than a piece of copper, but softer than steel, ankerite forms distinctive curved crystals. It is a rare mineral and is not mined for any specific purpose.

HARDNESS 3.5–4	SG 2.9
COLOUR Colourless to pale buff	
TRANSPARENCY Translucent	
LUSTRE Glassy to pearly	

RDNESS 3.5–4	SG 3.8
LOUR Rose-pink, brown or grey	
ANSPARENCY Transparent to translucent	
STRE Glassy to pearly	

Barytocalcite

This mineral is made up of barium and calcite. Its surface is covered in grooves and ridges that look like dog's teeth. It is often found within limestone and produces bubbles when put in hydrochloric acid.

HARDNESS 4	SG 3.7

COLOUR White, greyish, greenish, or yellowish

TRANSPARENCY Transparent to translucent

LUSTRE Glassy to resinous

Dolomite

This common mineral is recognized by its curved saddle-shaped crystals. It is an important rock-forming mineral and also a minor source of magnesium.

HARDNESS 3.5-4

SG 2.8-2.9

COLOUR Colourless, white, or cream

TRANSPARENCY Transparent to translucent

LUSTRE Glassy

Magnesite

It is almost impossible to melt magnesite, making it ideal for lining furnaces. It is also used in the production of synthetic rubber.

HARDNESS 4

SG 3

COLOUR White, light grey, yellowish, brownish

TRANSPARENCY Transparent to translucent

LUSTRE Glassy

Phosgenite

This rare carbonate forms close to Earth's surface when lead-rich minerals react with water. It is named after the colourless and poisonous gas phosgene, as they are both made up of carbon, oxygen, and chlorine.

HARDNESS 2.5–3	SG 6.1

COLOUR White, yellow, brown, or green

TRANSPARENCY Transparent to translucent

LUSTRE Resinous

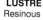

zurite

:urite takes its name from the
ersian *lazhudward*, meaning "blue". In
e 15th to 17th centuries, it was used as a natural
:louring pigment in European art. It is also one of
e sources of copper.

:ARDNESS 3.5–4

¡ 3.8

:OLOUR
ure to dark blue

RANSPARENCY
ansparent to
inslucent

JSTRE
assy to dull
earthy

Artinite

Artinite forms fluffy balls of
needle-shaped crystals. It dissolves in
cold acids, giving off water and carbon dioxide.

HARDNESS 2.5   **SG** 2

COLOUR White

TRANSPARENCY
Transparent

LUSTRE
Glassy

*Small
radiating
crystal*

trontianite

ie crystals of this mineral are short,
∍lumnar, and needle-shaped. It is the
ain source of strontium and is used in sugar
fining for extracting sugar from sugarcane.

:ARDNESS 3.5–4   **SG** 3.7

:OLOUR Colourless, grey, green,
llow, or reddish

RANSPARENCY
ansparent to
inslucent

JSTRE
assy

Trona

Trona takes it name from the Arabic *natrun*,
meaning "salt". It is usually found on the surface
of Earth in powdery form, especially in dry, salty
desert areas. It is also a source of sodium.

HARDNESS 2.5–3   **SG** 2.1

COLOUR Colourless to grey, yellow-white

TRANSPARENCY Transparent to translucent

LUSTRE Glassy, glistening

Phosphates, arsenates, and vanadates

These minerals are grouped together because they have similar patterns of atoms. The most abundant of the three are phosphates, with more than 200 known types.

Variscite

This mineral is named after Varisca, the old name for the German district of Voightland where variscite was first found. It is sometimes worn as jewellery, but it is porous and can absorb the body's natural oils, which discolour it.

HARDNESS 4.5	**SG** 2.6	
COLOUR Pale to apple-green		
TRANSPARENCY Opaque		
LUSTRE Glassy to waxy		

Pyromorphite

A minor ore of lead, this phosphate occurs in the oxidized zone of lead deposits. Pyromorphite gets its name from the Greek word *pyr*, meaning "fire", and *morphe*, meaning "form". It is so named because it forms crystals on cooling after being melted.

HARDNESS 3.5–4	**SG** 7	
COLOUR Green, yellow, orange, or brown		
TRANSPARENCY Transparent to translucent		
LUSTRE Resinous		

Wavellite

Radiating crystal

Wavellite contains a mixture of oxygen, aluminium, and phosphorus. It forms balls of crystals in chert rock, limestone, and granite. When these balls are broken, they reveal disclike patterns.

HARDNESS	3.5–4	SG	2.4

COLOUR Green or white

TRANSPARENCY Translucent

LUSTRE Glassy to resinous

Turquoise

One of the first gemstones to be mined, turquoise varies from sky-blue to green depending on the amount of iron or copper in it. Turquoise was the national gemstone of Persia (now Iran). The Persians believed that seeing the reflection of a new moon on a turquoise brought good luck.

HARDNESS	5–6	SG	2.6–2.8

COLOUR Blue, green

TRANSPARENCY Usually opaque

LUSTRE Waxy to dull

Apatite

Apatite is a name given to a group of minerals that contain calcium and phosphorus. It is used to make many things, including matches. Apatite derives its name from the Greek word *apate,* which means "deceit", because it looks similar to other minerals, including amethyst, aquamarine, and olivine.

HARDNESS	5
SG	3.1–3.2
COLOUR	Green, blue, violet, purple, colourless, yellow, or rose
TRANSPARENCY	Transparent to translucent
LUSTRE	Glassy, waxy

Carnotite

A radioactive mineral, carnotite is an important source of uranium, and gives off radium gas.

HARDNESS 2		**SG** 4.7	
COLOUR Yellow			
TRANSPARENCY Semi-transparent to opaque			
LUSTRE Pearly to dull			

Chalcophyllite

This mineral is named after the Greek words for "copper" and "leaf" because it contains copper and grows in a leaflike pattern. Easy to mould, copper has been cast since 4,000 BCE.

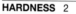

HARDNESS 2		**SG** 2.7	
COLOUR Vivid blue-green			
TRANSPARENCY Transparent to translucent			
LUSTRE Pearly to glassy			

Adamite

This mineral is generally highly fluorescent – when viewed under ultraviolet light, it gives off amazing colours. It has no commercial use but its bright and lustrous crystals are sought by mineral collectors.

HARDNESS 3.5	SG 4.4
	COLOUR Yellow, green, pink or violet
	TRANSPARENCY Transparent to translucent
	LUSTRE Glassy

Erythrite

This brightly coloured mineral is commonly called cobalt bloom. It is an ore of cobalt, nickel, and silver. Some of the best erythrite is found in Canada and Morocco.

HARDNESS 1.5–2.5

SG 3.1

COLOUR Purple-pink

TRANSPARENCY
Transparent to translucent

LUSTRE Diamondlike to glassy, pearly

Mimetite

Mimetite deposits are found where lead and arsenic occur together. Its name is derived from the Greek *mimetes*, meaning "imitator", because of its resemblance to pyromorphite.

HARDNESS 3.5–4

SG 7.3

COLOUR Pale yellow to yellowish-brown, orange, green

TRANSPARENCY Subtransparent

LUSTRE Resinous

This Aztec funeral mask is made of turquoise, gold, and shell overlaid on a **human skull**

Borax is the main source of boron, which is used in the manufacture of many essential products.

▲ Boron is added to many fertilizers as it helps plants to grow.

◀ Boron is one of the ingredients in some mouthwashes. It is also used as a disinfectant.

▲ Boron compounds from borax are an important component of many soaps.

Nitrates and borates

These minerals are formed when oxygen combines with nitrogen and boron respectively. They have low specific gravity and are usually soft.

Borax

The name borax comes from the Arabic *buraq*, which means "white". It is an evaporite mineral that forms in large desert lake beds, and contains sodium and boron. Borax can fuse or melt easily to become colourless glass, and is also a source of boron.

HARDNESS 2–2.5		**SG** 1.7	
COLOUR Colourless			
TRANSPARENCY Transparent to translucent			
LUSTRE Glassy to earthy			

Howlite

Howlite is named after its discoverer, Canadian chemist Henry How. It can be dyed and used in place of turquoise, although it is not as hard as turquoise and lacks depth of colour. Significant deposits of howlite are found in Death Valley, California, USA.

HARDNESS 3.5	**SG** 2.6
COLOUR White	
TRANSPARENCY Translucent to opaque	
LUSTRE Almost glassy	

Nitratine

Found in arid areas as a powderlike deposit on Earth's surface, nitratine is easily soluble in water and readily absorbs moisture from the air. It occurs mainly as huge grains and in crusts.

HARDNESS 1.5–2

SG 2.27

COLOUR White or colourless

TRANSPARENCY Transparent

LUSTRE Glassy

Sulphates, chromates, molybdates, tungstates

Oxygen combines with sulphur, chromium, molybdenum, and tungsten respectively to form these minerals. In their concentrated form they are valuable ores of the metal or semi-metal they contain

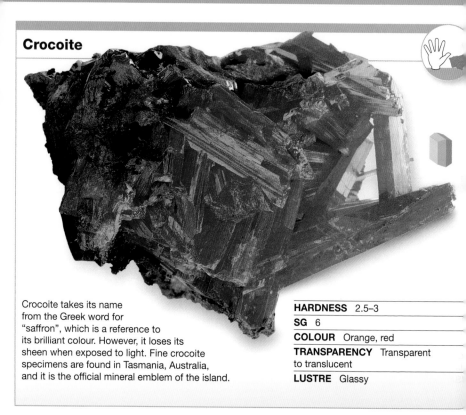

Crocoite

Crocoite takes its name from the Greek word for "saffron", which is a reference to its brilliant colour. However, it loses its sheen when exposed to light. Fine crocoite specimens are found in Tasmania, Australia, and it is the official mineral emblem of the island.

HARDNESS	2.5–3
SG	6
COLOUR	Orange, red
TRANSPARENCY	Transparent to translucent
LUSTRE	Glassy

GYPSUM

This common
sulphate is widely
used, especially in
building and design.

▲ Gypsum is used for making plaster
of Paris and mortar and also as an
adhesive in industrial processes.

▲ Alabaster, a fine-grained form
of gypsum, is used for carvings
and ornamental purposes.

Wulfenite

Named after mineralogist F X Wulfen, this
mineral is often found with lead ores and is
a minor source of molybdenum. Its unique
square-shaped crystals look like interlocking
plastic tiles. Large crystals come from Mexico,
USA, Zambia, China, and Slovenia.

HARDNESS 2.5–3		**SG** 6.5–7	
COLOUR Yellow, orange, red			
TRANSPARENCY Transparent to translucent			
LUSTRE Diamondlike to greasy			

Ferberite

Ferberite is named after German mineralogist Dr Moritz Rudolph Ferber. It is an iron tungstate that usually occurs as flat, stepped crystals, and is an ore of tungsten. This very useful metal is used in electric-light filaments.

HARDNESS 4–4.5	SG 7.5
COLOUR Black	
TRANSPARENCY Opaque	
LUSTRE Submetallic	

Chalcanthite

Gypsum

Gypsum is formed when seawater evaporates. Such surface-forming minerals are usually soft. An extremely common substance, gypsum is mined on a large scale in many parts of the world. Plaster of Paris, alabaster, fertilizers, and some types of explosives contain gypsum.

HARDNESS 2	SG 2.3
COLOUR Colourless, white, light brown, yellow, pink	
TRANSPARENCY Transparent to translucent	
LUSTRE Almost glassy to pearly	

halcanthite dissolves easily in water
nd is, therefore, more common in dry
gions. It used to be known as blue vitriol,
but is now named for the Greek words for
"copper" and "flower". It is an important
ore of copper especially in dry regions
such as Chile.

HARDNESS	2.5
SG	2.3
COLOUR	Blue
TRANSPARENCY	Transparent
LUSTRE	Glassy

Brochantite

This mineral is named after French
geologist A J M Brochant de Villiers. It is
a source of copper. The needle-like crystals
of brochantite are a few
millimetres long, but
magnificent specimens
10 mm long are
found in Namibia
and Arizona, USA.

HARDNESS	3.5–4	**SG**	4
COLOUR	Emerald-green		
TRANSPARENCY	Translucent		
LUSTRE	Glassy		

Scheelite

paque crystals of scheelite weighing
o to 7 kg (15 lb) are found in Arizona.
It is a major source of
tungsten. The nozzle
of the Saturn V rocket,
which launched *Apollo 11*
in 1969, was made of
tungsten-steel.

HARDNESS	4.5–5	**SG**	6.1
COLOUR	White, yellow, brown, green		
TRANSPARENCY	Transparent to translucent		
LUSTRE	Glassy to greasy		

Baryte

Also known as heavy spar, this mineral
gets its name from *barys,* the Greek word
for "heavy", because it has a high specific gravity.
It is the main source of barium, and is used in oil
and gas wells, in paper, and in cloth-making.

HARDNESS	3–3.5
SG	4.5
COLOUR	Colourless, white, grey, bluish, greenish, beige
TRANSPARENCY	Transparent to translucent
LUSTRE	Glassy, resinous, pearly

Silicates

The biggest group of minerals, silicates are found in abundance and are the main components of igneous and metamorphic rocks. Made of silicon and oxygen, they are usually hard, transparent, and are moderately dense.

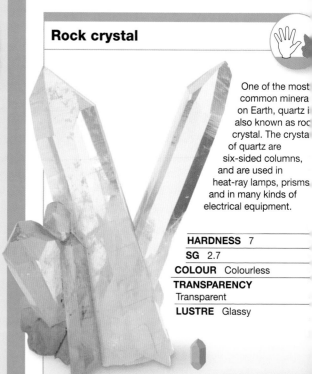

Rock crystal

One of the most common minera on Earth, quartz i also known as roc crystal. The crysta of quartz are six-sided columns, and are used in heat-ray lamps, prisms and in many kinds of electrical equipment.

HARDNESS	7
SG	2.7
COLOUR	Colourless
TRANSPARENCY	Transparent
LUSTRE	Glassy

Amethyst

Purple quartz is called amethyst, named after the maiden Amethyst from Greek mythology. Amethyst was very popular in 19th-century jewellery. Its colour comes from tiny quantities of iron in it. Some amethyst crystals turn yellow-brown when heated. These are often sold as citrine.

HARDNESS	7
SG	2.7
COLOUR	Violet
TRANSPARENCY	Opaque to translucent
LUSTRE	Glassy

Citrine

The name citrine comes from the Latin word *citrina,* meaning "yellow". It gets its colour from the iron oxide present in it. The mineral is also known as gold topaz.

HARDNESS	7
SG	2.7
COLOUR	Yellow, yellow-brown
TRANSPARENCY	Translucent to nearly opaque
LUSTRE	Glassy

Rose quartz

The pink variety of quartz is known as rose quartz. It has been carved since ancient times. Today, "crystal healers" believe that this mineral can bring unconditional love if worn against the skin.

HARDNESS	7	**SG**	2.65
COLOUR	Various, including pink and rose		
TRANSPARENCY	Translucent to nearly opaque		
LUSTRE	Glassy		

Agate

Agate is the banded variety of chalcedony, a fine-grained quartz. It usually grows in rings around a common centre, in rock cavities or extrusive igneous rocks.

HARDNESS 6.5–7	SG 2.6
COLOUR Colourless, white, yellow, grey, brown, blue, or red	
TRANSPARENCY Translucent to opaque	
LUSTRE Glassy to waxy	

Bloodstone

According to ancient Greek lore, bloodstone was a preserver of health and offered protection against nosebleeds, anger, and discord. Bloodstones are named for their red spots, which resemble drops of blood.

HARDNESS 6.5–7	SG 2.6
	COLOUR Different colours with red spots
	TRANSPARENCY Translucent to opaque
	LUSTRE Glassy

Onyx

Onyx is the striped, semiprecious variety of agate with alternating bands of colour. The layers of contrasting colours make it an ideal material for carving jewellery.

Translucent brown sard

HARDNESS 6.5–7	
SG 2.6	
COLOUR Different colours	
TRANSPARENCY Translucent to nearly opaque	
LUSTRE Glassy	

Onyx builds up in layers of silica deposits, which form bands of different colours

Opal

Opal occurs in many forms and many different crystal shapes. It is used as a semiprecious gemstone, and is chiefly found in Australia.

HARDNESS 5–6	SG 1.9–2.3

COLOUR Colourless, white, yellow, orange, rose-red, black, or dark blue

TRANSPARENCY Transparent to translucent

LUSTRE Glassy

Sard

A translucent mineral, sard has been used since ancient times for making cameos and jewellery. It was used at Harappa, one of the oldest centres of the Indus civilization (c. 2,300–1,500 BCE).

HARDNESS 6.5–7	SG 2.6

COLOUR Light to dark-brown

TRANSPARENCY Translucent to opaque

LUSTRE Glassy

Lazurite

This rare mineral forms in limestone and it is the main mineral in lapis lazuli – a rock prized for its use in carvings, medicines, cosmetics, and jewellery for thousands of years. Lazurite is also the main ingredient of a brilliant blue pigment called ultramarine. The best lazurite crystals come from Afghanistan.

HARDNESS 5–5.5	**SG** 2.4	
COLOUR Various intense shades of blue		
TRANSPARENCY Translucent to opaque		
LUSTRE Dull to glassy		

Leucite

The Greek word *leukos*, meaning "white", gives leucite its name – a reference to its most common colour. Leucite occurs only in igneous rocks, mainly those that are potassium-rich and silica-poor.

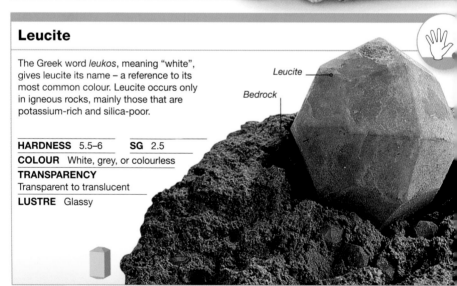

Leucite

Bedrock

HARDNESS 5.5–6	**SG** 2.5
COLOUR White, grey, or colourless	
TRANSPARENCY Transparent to translucent	
LUSTRE Glassy	

Orthoclase

A major rock-forming mineral, orthoclase's pink crystals give granite its characteristic colour. This mineral is important in ceramics, where it is used as a clay for making objects and as a glaze. Moonstone, the smooth and shiny variety of orthoclase, was regarded as sacred in India.

HARDNESS 6	**SG** 2.5–2.6

COLOUR Colourless, white, cream, yellow, pink, brown-red

TRANSPARENCY Transparent to translucent

LUSTRE Glassy

Cancrinite

This silicate was found originally in the Ural Mountains in Russia. It forms in a number of igneous rocks. Cancrinite rarely forms crystals, although they may grow to several centimetres wide.

HARDNESS 5–6	**SG** 2.5

COLOUR Pale to dark yellow, orange, violet, pink, or purple

TRANSPARENCY Transparent to translucent

LUSTRE Glassy

Topaz

This mineral's name was probably inspired by the Sanskrit word *tapas*, which means "fire" – a reference to its golden-yellow colour. Topaz also exists in other colours. It is classified as a gemstone because of its beautiful and rare crystals.

HARDNESS	8	SG	3.4–3.6

COLOUR Colourless, blue, yellow, pink, brown, green

TRANSPARENCY Transparent to translucent

LUSTRE Glassy

Grossular

Zircon

This mineral often matches diamond in its sparkling brilliance. Some crystals of zircon found in Mount Narryer in western Australia are almost 4.4 billion years old.

HARDNESS	7.5	SG	4.6–4.7

COLOUR Colourless, brown, red, yellow, orange, blue, green

TRANSPARENCY Transparent to opaque

LUSTRE Diamondlike to oily

Kyanite

This silicate has been used to make heat-resistant porcelains, such as used in spark plugs. Gem-quality kyanite crystals are found in Bahia, Brazil. Its name is an adaptation of the Greek word *kyanos*, meaning "dark blue" – a reference to one of its many colour forms.

HARDNESS	4.5–6
SG	3.6
COLOUR	Blue, green

TRANSPARENCY Transparent to translucent

LUSTRE Glassy

This type of garnet is commonly found in calcium-rich metamorphic rocks, and has been found in meteorites. Green grossular, also known as tsavolite, comes from Tanzania.

HARDNESS 6.5–7

SG 3.6

COLOUR Wide range of colours

TRANSPARENCY Transparent to translucent

LUSTRE Glassy

Andalusite

Andalusite is usually found in metamorphic rocks. Sometimes its crystals grow together trapping dark, carbon-based matter in between, which forms a cross when seen in cross-section.

HARDNESS 6.5–7.5   **SG** 3.2

COLOUR Pink, brown, white, grey, violet, yellow, green, blue

TRANSPARENCY Transparent to nearly opaque

LUSTRE Glassy

Sillimanite

This is named after Professor Benjamin Silliman, a geologist, chemist, and founder of the *American Journal of Science.* Sillimanite is commonly used to make heat-resistant porcelain.

HARDNESS 7

SG 3.2–3.3

COLOUR Colourless, white, pale yellow, blue, green, violet

TRANSPARENCY Transparent to translucent

LUSTRE Silky

Olivine

Olivine refers to a group of silicate minerals that form in molten rock beneath Earth's surface. The ancient Greeks and Romans were among the first people to use these minerals for decoration. Peridot is the gem-quality variety of olivine.

HARDNESS 6.5–7	**SG** 3.3–4.3

COLOUR Green, yellow, brown, white, or black

TRANSPARENCY
Transparent to translucent

LUSTRE Glassy

Natrolite

Natrolite takes its name from the Greek *natrium*, which means "soda" – a reference to its sodium content. It is found in cavities, volcanic ash deposits, and as veins in some rocks.

HARDNESS 5–5.5

SG 2.3

COLOUR Pale pink, colourless, white, grey, red, yellow, or green

TRANSPARENCY Transparent to translucent

LUSTRE Glassy to pearly

Scapolite

Previously known as wernerite and dipyre, this silicate is known for its large crystals. The largest ones usually grow in marble.

HARDNESS 5–6 | **SG** 2.5– 2.7

COLOUR Colourless, white, grey, yellow, orange, or pink

TRANSPARENCY Transparent to opaque

LUSTRE Glassy

The gold throne in Topkapi Palace, Istanbul, is decorated with 955 peridots.

Diopside

Diopside is found in metamorphic rocks that were once limestones or dolomites, and in some igneous rocks such as kimberlite. The mineral occurs in the rocks of the Tyrol mountains in Austria and Italy, and in the USA.

HARDNESS 6

SG 3.3

COLOUR White, pale to dark green, violet-blue

TRANSPARENCY Transparent to translucent

LUSTRE Glassy

Rhodonite

This silicate was named for its colour from the Greek word *rhodon*, meaning "rose". Rhodonite is widely used in making beads and jewellery, even though it is fragile and has to be carefully polished.

HARDNESS 6	**SG** 3.5–3.7
COLOUR Pink to rose-red	
TRANSPARENCY Translucent	
LUSTRE Glassy	

Jadeite

Jadeite is one of the two minerals that are commonly called jade. The other variety is nephrite. For the ancient Indians, jadeite was a symbol of life, and regarded as precious as gold. Burma (Myanmar) is a major source of the mineral and ancient jadeite tools have been found there.

HARDNESS 6–7	**SG** 3.2–3.4
COLOUR White, green, lilac, pink, brown, orange, yellow, red, blue, or black	
TRANSPARENCY Transparent to translucent	
LUSTRE Glassy to greasy	

Augite

This mineral is commonly found in dark-coloured igneous rocks. It also occurs in some metamorphic rocks and meteorites, and can even be found on the Moon.

HARDNESS 5.5–6	**SG** 3.3
COLOUR Greenish-black to black, dark green, brown	
TRANSPARENCY Translucent to nearly opaque	
LUSTRE Glassy to dull	

Richterite

Richterite is a rare manganese stone usually found in igneous rocks and limestones. It was named after the German mineralogist Theodore Richter in 1865. It is mainly used for decorative purposes.

HARDNESS 5–6

SG 3–3.5

COLOUR Brown, yellow, red, or green

TRANSPARENCY Transparent to translucent

LUSTRE Glassy

Hornblende

Recent studies have discovered that hornblende is a group of minerals and not a single form of a mineral. However, only detailed analysis can tell them all apart. Hornblende may occur with ruby in the Harts Range mountains in Australia.

HARDNESS 5–6

SG 3.1–3.3

COLOUR Green, black

TRANSPARENCY Translucent to opaque

LUSTRE Glassy

Nephrite

Nephrite's tight interlocking fibres make it a hard rock, suitable for carving. It is named after the Latin word *nephrus*, meaning "kidney", as it was used to treat kidney diseases.

HARDNESS 6.5

SG 2.9–3.4

COLOUR Cream, light to dark green

TRANSPARENCY Translucent to nearly opaque

LUSTRE Dull to waxy

Riebeckite

This mineral was once valued for its fireproofing qualities and its ability to withstand electricity and acid, but scientists later discovered that the fibres are harmful to people and caused diseases.

HARDNESS 6

SG 3.3–3.4

COLOUR Dark blue, black

TRANSPARENCY Transparent to translucent

LUSTRE Glassy, silky

Emerald

The green variety of the mineral beryl is known as emerald. To the Egyptians, it was a symbol of fertility and life. The finest emeralds, such as those in the British Crown Jewels, come from Colombia, where they have been mined for centuries.

HARDNESS 7.5–8

SG 2.6–3

COLOUR Green

TRANSPARENCY Transparent to translucent

LUSTRE Glassy

Cordierite

This mineral was named after French geologist Pierre L A Cordier. Gem-quality cordierite is also called "water sapphire" after its blue colour.

HARDNESS 7–7.5   **SG** 2.6

COLOUR Blue, blue-green, grey-violet

TRANSPARENCY Transparent to translucent

LUSTRE Glassy to greasy

Vesuvianite

The crystals of vesuvianite are cut and polished for collectors but the transparent variety is too soft to wear. It forms when limestone undergoes changes due to heat and pressure.

HARDNESS 6.5

SG 3.4

COLOUR Green, yellow

TRANSPARENCY Transparent to translucent

LUSTRE Glassy to resinous

Hemimorphite

Rounded masses, usually colourless

Hemimorphite gets its name from the Greek *hemi*, meaning "half", and *morphe,* meaning "form", which is a reference to its unique crystal form. The two ends of each crystal are of different shapes, which is quite rare in minerals.

HARDNESS 4.5–5	SG 3.4–3.5
COLOUR Colourless, white, yellow, blue, or green	
TRANSPARENCY Transparent to translucent	
LUSTRE Glassy	

Talc

One of Earth's softest minerals, talc is ground finely to make talcum powder. It is the main ingredient of soapstone and has been traditionally carved to make ornaments. Talc is also used in paints and for making paper.

HARDNESS 1	SG 2.8

COLOUR White, colourless, green, yellow to brown

TRANSPARENCY Translucent

LUSTRE Pearly to greasy

Muscovite

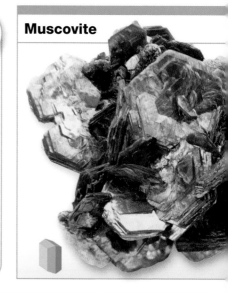

Pyrophyllite

The name of this mineral is based on the Greek words for "fire" and "leaf" because it sheds thin, leaflike layers when heated. It provides a sheen to lipsticks and is also used as a filler in paints and rubber and in dusting powders. The ancient Chinese carved it into small images and ornaments.

HARDNESS 1–2	SG 2.7–2.9

COLOUR White, colourless, brown-green, pale blue, grey

TRANSPARENCY Transparent to translucent

LUSTRE Pearly to dull

Muscovite forms flat sheets and, though it looks brittle, is a tough mineral. It is also called isinglass – a reference to its use in window panes in Russia. It is a member of the mica group of minerals.

HARDNESS 2.5

SG 2.8

COLOUR Colourless, silver-white, pale green, rose, brown

TRANSPARENCY Transparent to translucent

LUSTRE Glassy

Biotite

Biotite is also called black mica because of its iron content and dark colour. It is abundant in igneous and metamorphic rocks. Like muscovite, it splits into thin sheets.

HARDNESS 2.5–3   **SG** 2.7–3.4

COLOUR Black, brown, pale yellow, tan, or bronze

TRANSPARENCY Transparent to translucent

LUSTRE Glassy to submetallic

Serpentine

There are 16 varieties of serpentine, which is named for its snakeskin-like texture. Serpentine was carved into vases and bowls on the island of Crete by the Minoans around 3,000–1,100 BCE.

HARDNESS 3.5–5.5

SG 2.5–2.6

COLOUR White, grey, yellow, green, or greenish-blue

TRANSPARENCY Translucent to opaque

LUSTRE Glassy to greasy, resinous, earthy, dull

Chrysocolla

Fine texture

The Greek philosopher Theophrastus used the term "chrysocolla" to refer to various materials used to bind together pieces of gold. *Chrysos* is "gold" and *kola* is "glue" in Greek. The mineral is found worldwide.

HARDNESS	2–4	SG	2–2.4

COLOUR Blue, blue-green

TRANSPARENCY Translucent to nearly opaque

LUSTRE Glassy to earthy

Apophyllite

Once thought to be a single mineral, apophyllite is now known to have two varieties. Both separate into layers when heated. Colourless and green specimens from India are sometimes cut and polished as collector's gems. Crystals up to 20 cm (8 in) long are found in Bento Gonsalves, Brazil.

Blocklike crystals

HARDNESS 4.5–5

SG 2.3–2.4

COLOUR Colourless pink, green, or yellow

TRANSPARENCY Transparent to translucent

LUSTRE Glassy

Prehnite

Named after its discoverer Hendrik von Prehn, a Dutch military officer, prehnite is often found lining cavities in volcanic rocks. It is commonly found with the mineral zeolite and the two may be confused with one another. Transparent prehnite from Australia and Scotland is a collector's item. It is also sold under the name Cape emerald.

HARDNESS 6–6.5   **SG** 2.9

COLOUR Green, yellow, tan, or white

TRANSPARENCY Transparent to translucent

LUSTRE Glassy

Organic gems

Organic gems form when living things or the substances they give off fossilize over a long period of time. They are softer than rock gems and so have been used as decorative items since ancient times.

FOCUS ON...
PEARLS
Different types of pea form depending on the shellfish and its environment.

Amber

Amber is the fossilized resin or sap of conifer trees. Sometimes it contains trapped insects. Mostly transparent, some pieces of amber are cloudy due to the air trapped inside. Its softness allows it to be carved into jewellery.

HARDNESS	2–2.5
SG	1.1
COLOUR	Yellow, sometimes brownish or reddish
TRANSPARENCY	Transparent to translucent
LUSTRE	Resinous

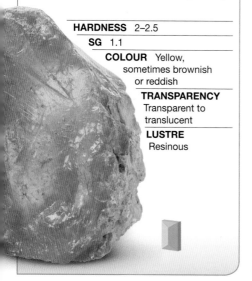

Coral

Coral comes from the skeletons of tiny sea animals. It can be polished to bring out its beautiful colours, and is easily carved into figures or beads. The most valuable coral is red.

HARDNESS	3.5	**SG**	2.6-2.7
COLOUR Red, pink, black, blue, golden			
TRANSPARENCY Opaque			
LUSTRE Dull to glassy			

Freshwater pearls come from ssels. They are attached to shell and so are flat on one e when removed.

▲ Marine-cultured pearls are grown in the sea using oyster shells and often have uniform shapes and sizes.

▲ Mother of pearl is a hard layer that lines the insides of some shellfish. It has been used for making utensils for a long time.

Shell

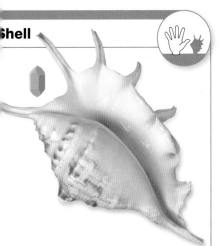

This is a hard covering found on many molluscs. hells are made of calcite, which shellfish take from sea water. They are used in inlays, eads, and in other decorative items.

HARDNESS 2.5	SG About 1.3
COLOUR Red, pink, brown, blue, golden	
RANSPARENCY Translucent to opaque	
USTRE Dull to glassy	

Pearl

Pearl forms in certain shellfish, especially oysters. Gem-quality pearls come from oysters of tropical seas. The best and the most valuable pearls are perfectly round, but many are egg- or pear-shaped.

HARDNESS 3	SG 2.7
COLOUR White, cream, black, blue, yellow, green, or pink	
TRANSPARENCY Opaque	
LUSTRE Pearly	

Blister pearls

Dominican amber is around
25 million years old

AMBER
Resin from trees often traps insects and plant remains, which may become fossilized over time as the resin hardens into amber. Fossil remains found in Dominican amber can help us to understand the ecosystem of the tropical forests that existed long ago.

The periodic table

Minerals and rocks are made up of elements – pure, naturally occurring substances that cannot be broken down further. Each element is made up of atoms. The atoms in different elements contain different amounts of particles called protons, neutrons, and electrons, which affects their chemistry. Elements are arranged in a system called the periodic table according to their chemical and physical properties.

Alkali metals are very reactive

Alkaline earth metals are commonly found in rocks

The Lanthanide and Actinide series contain some important radioactive minerals, such as uranium

Transition metals include many of Earth's most common metals

This is the atomic number of the element, which is the number of protons in each atom

This is the unique symbol for the element

26
Fe
Iron

1 **H** Hydrogen								
3 **Li** Lithium	4 **Be** Beryllium							
11 **Na** Sodium	12 **Mg** Magnesium							
19 **K** Potassium	20 **Ca** Calcium	21 **Sc** Scandium	22 **Ti** Titanium	23 **V** Vanadium	24 **Cr** Chromium	25 **Mn** Manganese	26 **Fe** Iron	27 **Co** Cobalt
37 **Rb** Rubidium	38 **Sr** Strontium	39 **Y** Yttrium	40 **Zr** Zirconium	41 **Nb** Niobium	42 **Mo** Molybdenum	43 **Tc** Technetium	44 **Ru** Ruthenium	45 **Rh** Rhodium
55 **Cs** Caesium	56 **Ba** Barium	57–71 Lanthanide series	72 **Hf** Hafnium	73 **Ta** Tantalum	74 **W** Tungsten	75 **Re** Rhenium	76 **Os** Osmium	77 **Ir** Iridium
87 **Fr** Francium	88 **Ra** Radium	89–103 Actinide series	104 **Rf** Rutherfordium	105 **Db** Dubnium	106 **Sg** Seaborgium	107 **Bh** Bohrium	108 **Hs** Hassium	109 **Mt** Meitnerium

elements with
similar properties
are grouped together
in the periodic table.
Scientists can tell
what an element is
like from its position
in the table.

Alkali metals

Alkaline earth
metals

Transition metals

Lanthanide series

Actinide series

Other metals

Semi-metals

Non-metals

Noble gases

Hydrogen

Unknown
chemistry

Noble gases almost never
react with other elements

Semi-metals sit
between the metals
and non-metals

Non-metals
are generally dull
and break easily

					2 **He** Helium
5 **B** Boron	6 **C** Carbon	7 **N** Nitrogen	8 **O** Oxygen	9 **F** Fluorine	10 **Ne** Neon
13 **Al** Aluminium	14 **Si** Silicon	15 **P** Phosphorus	16 **S** Sulphur	17 **Cl** Chlorine	18 **Ar** Argon

Other metals include many
important elements, such
as aluminium and lead

28 **Ni** Nickel	29 **Cu** Copper	30 **Zn** Zinc	31 **Ga** Gallium	32 **Ge** Germanium	33 **As** Arsenic	34 **Se** Selenium	35 **Br** Bromine	36 **Kr** Krypton
46 **Pd** Palladium	47 **Ag** Silver	48 **Cd** Cadmium	49 **In** Indium	50 **Sn** Tin	51 **Sb** Antimony	52 **Te** Tellurium	53 **I** Iodine	54 **Xe** Xenon
78 **Pt** Platinum	79 **Au** Gold	80 **Hg** Mercury	81 **Tl** Thallium	82 **Pb** Lead	83 **Bi** Bismuth	84 **Po** Polonium	85 **At** Astatine	86 **Rn** Radon
110 **Ds** Darmstadtium	111 **Rg** Roentgenium	112 **Cn** Copernicium	113 **Uut** Ununtrium	114 **Uuq** Ununquadium	115 **Uup** Ununpentium	116 **Uuh** Ununhexium	117 **Uus** Ununseptium	118 **Uuo** Ununoctium

Rock facts

LANDMARK ROCK FORMATIONS

▶ The **Rock of Gibraltar** is a huge mass of limestone at the southern tip of Spain. It rises 426 m (1,400 ft) above the sea.

▶ **Shiprock Pinnacle** in New Mexico is the remains of a 27-million-year-old volcanic vent that stands 500 m (1,640 ft) above the surrounding plain. It is considered sacred by the Navajo people.

▶ **Giant's Causeway** in Northern Ireland is a collection of 40,000 basalt pillars formed 50–60 million years ago. The tallest pillars can measure up to 25 m (82 ft) high.

▶ **Ayer's Rock**, or **Uluru**, in Australia is a giant outcrop of ancient sandstone that stands 348 m (1,142 ft) high and measures 9.4 km (5.8 miles) around its base.

▶ **Delicate Arch**, in Utah, USA, formed from weathered sandstone that has naturally eroded into a graceful arch that is 13.5 m (45 ft) high and wide enough to drive trucks through.

METEORITES

Around 20,000 meteorites fall from space to Earth every year. Most are small, but some larger ones weigh many tonnes.

• **Willamette meteorite** landed in Oregon, USA, in 1906. It weighed more than 14.2 tonnes – more than the weight of three elephants.

• **Zagami meteorite** landed in Nigeria in 1962. It weighed 18 kg (40 lb) and is the largest meteorite from Mars ever found on Earth. It started as a chunk of volcanic rock on Mars that was flung into space about 2.5 million years ago when an asteroid or comet hit Mars.

A typical meteorite enters Earth's atmosphere at 10–70 km (6.2–43.5 miles) per second.

• **Y000593 meteorite** landed in Antarctica in 2000. It weighed 13.7 kg (30.2 lb), about the same as 240 eggs.

• **Sayh al Uhaymir 008** landed in Oman in 1999. It weighed 8.5 kg (18.7 lb) – as much as a small dog.

• **Nakhla meteorite** landed in El-Nakhla village, Egypt, in 1911. It weighed 5 kg (11 lb) – as much as five bags of sugar.

OCK ELEMENTS

re than 98 per cent of all rocks in the
rld are formed from a combination of
eight elements.

ement	% of all rocks
ygen	46.5
con	27.6
minium	8
n	5
cium	3 .6
dium	2.8
tassium	2.6
gnesium	2
tal	**98.1%**

ILDING WITH ROCK

arge building, such as a bank or town
l, can be like a rock museum – it's a
nce to see how useful rocks are in
ryday life.

Granite can be used for the base
walls because it is very tough.

The columns and steps of
trances are often made with
ite **limestone**.

Important buildings often
ve floors of **marble**
cause it looks beautiful
en polished.

CLAY

Clay is a versatile sedimentary rock that
is used for much more than just pots.

♦ Clay is used to make ceramic tiles,
pottery, porcelain, baths, sinks, drainpipes,
bricks, and also firebricks for chimneys
and furnaces.

♦ It is used in textiles to give weight
to the fabric, and in paper-making to
give paper a gloss.

♦ Wild macaws often peck on clay at
riverbanks. It helps them to digest the
poisons in some of the seeds they eat.

♦ Elephants lick clay from mud holes.
This helps them to digest leaves they
have eaten during the day.

♦ Kaolinite is a type of clay used in many
indigestion remedies for people.

♦ Clay helps soil to retain the fertilizer
chemicals it obtains from manure,
and also helps plants to grow by
absorbing ammonia and other
gases. However, too much
clay will make the soil
heavy, preventing water
and air from seeping in.

Most rocks are hard
and stiff, but a few are
flexible. A rare type
of sandstone found in
India can be bent
in your hands.

♦ Fuller's earth is a clay
material used to purify fats.

Mineral facts

MOST VALUABLE DIAMONDS

Koh-i-Noor is the largest and purest diamond in the world. It weighs 109 carats (21.8 g/0.77 oz) and is considered priceless.

The **Sancy diamond** was once owned by the Great Mughals of India. This priceless diamond weighs 55.23 carats (11.05 g/0.39 oz).

The **Cullinan** diamond is valued at $400 million. It was found in 1905 and weighed 3,106.75 carats (621.35 g/ 21.9 oz) before being cut into 9 large and 96 smaller stones.

The **Hope diamond** weighs 45.52 carats (9.1 g/0.32 oz) and is worth $350 million – but is said to bring bad luck.

MINING FOR MINERALS

- The earliest mines were small pits and tunnels that were dug about 8,000 years ago. They were mines for flint, a rock used to make tools, spears, and arrowheads.

- The first mines for metal were dug about 5,500 years ago. Tin and copper ores were crushed and heated together to make bronze.

- The deepest mines are the gold mines of South Africa. The record holder is Western Deep Levels Mine. Some of its tunnels are 3.5 km (2.2 miles) below the surface.

- Not all mines are holes in the ground. Along the coast of Namibia, Africa, large ships vacuum up sand from the ocean floor and sift it for diamonds.

HEALING MINERALS

People have believed for thousands of years that the crystals of certain minerals can help heal the body and calm the mind, and bring good luck.

Rose quartz brings unconditional love.

Lapis lazuli promotes friendship.

Jade brings relaxation.

Bloodstone increases creativity and intuition

Onyx changes bad habits.

Hematite relieves the stress of air travel.

Amethyst cures acne.

SEFUL MINERALS

nerals make up 99 per cent of Earth's ust. Many are valuable and are used to ake items that we need every day.

Aluminium is the most abundant metal und in minerals, including **bauxite** and **bbite**. It is used to make cans d in the construction of buildings.

Antimony comes from the mineral **ibnite**. It is used to harden d in batteries and cables, and make fireworks and glass.

Chromite is a source the metal chromium, ich is used to harden el and make machine ols, ball bearings, and chen utensils.

Copper is used in electric res and cables, in plumbing and kitchen utensils. It is also used make alloys such as brass (a mixture copper and zinc) and bronze (copper d tin). **Chalcopyrite** is the main urce of copper.

Feldspar is the one of Earth's most mmon minerals. It is used in making ass and ceramics, and in soaps, abrasives, ment, and concrete.

★ **Fluorspar** is used to make acid for the production of non-stick coatings on pans. It is also used in toothpaste.

★ Iron is a metal found in minerals such as **hematite**. It is used to make steel, magnets, and car parts.

★ Lead is a metal found in the mineral **galena** and is used to make batteries and television tubes.

There are more than 4,500 known minerals in the world. Only 100 are common – the rest are rarer than gold.

★ Limestone is a rock made mostly of the mineral **calcite**. It is used in the construction of buildings and in making cement, paper, plastic, and glass.

★ Manganese is used in making steel, and in dyes, alloys, and batteries. It is obtained from ore minerals including **pyrolusite**.

★ **Mica** is a group of important minerals that are used in paints, plastics, and rubber.

★ **Nickel** is a native element that is used to make stainless steel.

★ The native element **silver** is used to make jewellery, cutlery, and coins.

GLOSSARY

Acid A chemical that contains a reactive form of the hydrogen atom. This readily attacks other chemicals.

Atom The basic unit of an element.

Adamantine lustre A particularly brilliant shine as shown by diamond.

Asteroid A chunk of rock smaller than a planet that orbits the Sun.

Atmosphere The blanket of gases surrounding Earth or another planet.

Bed A thin layer of sedimentary rock.

Breccia A sedimentary rock made up of angular fragments.

Canyon A deep, steep-sided valley, typically cut by a river.

Carat The standard measure of weight for precious stones and metals. A carat is equal to 0.2 g (0.007 oz).

Chondrite A stony meteorite containing tiny granules of pyroxene and olivine.

Cleavage The way a mineral or rock breaks along a certain plane, or in a certain direction.

Concretions Usually rounded, rock masses formed and found in beds of shale or clay.

Core Earth's hot, dense iron-rich centre – liquid on the outside and solid on the inside.

Crystal A naturally occurring substance whose atoms are arranged in a regular manner.

Crystal system The systems into which crystals are grouped based on their symmetry. There are six crystal systems: cubic, monoclinic, triclinic, trigonal/hexagonal, orthorhombic, and tetragonal.

Crust Earth's rigid, outermost layer. It is divided into thicker, older continental crust (mainly granite) and thinner, more recent oceanic crust (mainly basalt).

Detrital A type of sediment that has settled in water or has been deposited by water.

Dull lustre A shine that reflects very little.

Dyke A thin, sheetlike igneous intrusion that cuts across older rock structures.

Dynamic pressure The process by which an existing rock changes due to pressure alone to form metamorphic rocks.

Earthy lustre A non-reflective mineral lustre.

Element A substance that cannot be broken down further.

Erosion A slow process in which rocks are worn away by moving water, ice, and wind.

Eruption A discharge of lava, ash, or gas from a volcanic cone or vent.

Evaporite A natural salt or mineral left behind after the water it was dissolved in has dried up.

Extrusive rock A rock that forms when lava flows onto Earth's surface, cools, and solidifies.

Faces The external flat surfaces that make up a crystal's shape.

Fault An extended fracture in rock along which rock masses move.

Fluorescence The op[tical] effect whereby a mine[ral] appears a different col[our] in ultraviolet light than ordinary daylight.

Foliation A pattern formed when different minerals separate with[in] a metamorphic rock.

Fold Bends in rock strata (layers) caused by the movement of tectonic plates.

Fossil Any record of p[ast] life preserved in rocks, including bones, shells, footprints, and dung.

Fracture The distinctiv[e] way in which a mineral breaks.

Gemstone A mineral, usually crystal-like, wh[ich] is valued for its colour, rarity, and hardness.

Geologist A scientist who studies Earth and structure and composit[ion].

Groundmass Compac[t] fine-grained mineral material in which larger crystals are embedded.

Habit The general shape of a mineral.

Hydrothermal vein A crack in rock through which hot mineral wate[r] circulate due to volcan[ic] activity. As the waters cool, minerals start to crystallize, forming gemstones and ores.

trusive rock A rock that forms when magma solidifies below Earth's crust.

Igneous rock A rock formed from solidification of lava or magma on or below Earth's surface.

descence A play of colours that looks like oil on water that occurs when light reflects off internal elements of a rock or mineral.

Lava Magma that has flowed onto Earth's surface through a volcanic opening.

Lustre The way in which light reflects off the surface of a mineral.

Magma Molten rock found deep inside Earth.

Mantle The middle layer of Earth, between the core and the crust. It consists of hot, dense rocks, such as peridotite.

Metallic lustre A shine like that of polished metal.

Metamorphic rock A rock formed when other rocks are transformed by heat, pressure, or both.

Meteor A meteoroid (rock and dust debris in space) that enters Earth's atmosphere and appears as a shooting star.

Meteorite A meteoroid that reaches the surface of Earth.

Mineral A naturally occurring solid with specific characteristics, such as a particular chemical composition and crystal shape.

Mineralogist A scientist who studies minerals.

Native element A chemical element found in nature in its pure form.

Nodule A hard, rounded, stony lump found in sedimentary rock, typically made from calcite, silica, pyrite, or gypsum.

Oolitic A rock that forms from ooliths, which are individual round grains of sediment. Most ooliths are made of calcite.

Opaque A substance or material that does not let light pass through it.

Ore A rock or mineral from which a metal can be extracted.

Organic Relating to living things.

Prism A solid geometric figure with a set of faces parallel to one another.

Pluton Any body of intrusive igneous rock.

Quarry A place where stone is dug up.

Regional change The process by which an existing rock changes due to heat and pressure to form metamorphic rocks.

Resinous lustre A shine like that of resin.

Rock A solid mixture of minerals. There are three types: igneous, metamorphic, and sedimentary.

Secondary mineral A mineral that replaces another as a result of weathering or other alteration process.

Sediments Particles of rock, mineral, or organic matter that are carried by wind, water, and ice.

Sedimentary rock A rock formed from sediments that have been cemented together by weathering or burial.

Semi-metal A chemical element that shares some properties with metals and some with non-metals.

Sill A thin, sheetlike, igneous intrusion that forms between layers of existing rocks.

Specific gravity The ratio of a mineral's weight compared to the weight of an equal volume of water.

Streak The colour of a mineral's powder. It is less variable than the colour of mineral, so is a more reliable identification tool.

Tectonic plate One of about 12 huge, floating rock slabs that make up the rigid outer layer of Earth's crust.

Thermal contact The process by which an existing rock changes due to heat alone to form metamorphic rock.

Uplift The result of rock structures being raised upwards by the movement of tectonic plates. Sediments formed on the sea bed may be uplifted to become mountains.

Vitreous lustre A shine like that of glass.

Volcano The site of an eruption of lava and hot gases from within Earth. Magma flows up a central passage and erupts as lava.

Weathering The slow breakdown of rock by long exposure to the weather, including moisture, frost, and rainwater.

Index

M

magma 4, 15, 16, 17, 18, 20, 57
magnesite 108
magnetite 7, 94
malachite 55, 60, 106
manganese 149
mantle, Earth's 4
marble 19, 42, 43, 104, 105
marcasite 84–5
megagems 67
mercury 73, 76
metamorphic minerals 57
metamorphic rocks 8, 9, 16, 17, 19, 42–9
meteorites 52–3, 146
mica 61
micaceous sandstone 38
migmatite 47
millerite 83
millet-seed sandstone 19
mimetite 113
mineralogists 7
minerals 54–143
  composition of 6
  facts 148–9
  formation of 56–7
  groups 7, 58–61
  identifying 62–5
  useful 149
mining 7, 148
Mohs' scale 64
molybdates 61, 118–21
molybdenite 65, 87
muscovite 136–7
mylonite 48

N

Nakhla meteorite 146
native elements 58, 68–75, 149
natrolite 61, 131
nephrite 133
nickel 149
nickel-iron 72
nitrates 60, 116–17
nitratine 117
nodules 39

O

obsidian 9, 20, 62
oil 7
olivine 8, 9, 57, 130–1
onyx 124–5, 148
opal 67, 122, 125
ore minerals 7, 59, 98
ores 92–3
organic gems 67, 140–3
organic minerals 61
orpiment 65, 84
orthoclase 127
oxides 59, 92–7

P

pearl 61, 67, 140–1
peat 32
pegmatite 27
Pélé's hair 24–5
pentlandite 78
peridot 130, 131
peridotite 18, 23
periodic table 144–5
perovskite 95

phonolite 22, 29
phosgenite 108
phosphates 60, 110–13
phyllite 42
pink granite 18
plagioclase feldspar 8
platinum 69, 76
pluton 16
polishing 66
polybasite 90
porphyry 27
precious gems 67
prehnite 139
pressure 16, 17, 19, 42, 57
proustite 58, 90, 91
pumice 24
pyrargyrite 91
pyrite 58, 84–5
pyrochlore 97
pyrolusite 149
pyromorphite 110
pyrophyllite 136
pyroxene 8, 9
pyrrhotite 79

QR

quartz 58, 61, 64, 65, 122, 123
quartzite 44–5
realgar 80
record keeping 11
red sandstone 9
regional change 17
rhodochrosite 106–7
rhodonite 132
rhomb porphyry 27
rhyolite 22–3
richterite 133

Acknowledgements

Dorling Kindersley would like to thank: Monica Byles for proofreading; Helen Peters for indexing; David Roberts and Rob Campbell for database creation; Claire Bowers, Fabian Harry, Romaine Werblow, and Rose Horridge for DK Picture Library assistance; Ritu Mishra, Nasreen Habib, and Neha Chaudhary for editorial assistance; and Isha Nagar for design assistance.

The publishers would also like to thank the following for their kind permission to reproduce their photographs:

(Key: a-above; b-below/bottom; c-centre; f-far; l-left; r-right; t-top)

2–3 Corbis: Walter Geiersperger (c). 5 Getty Images: Toshi Sasaki / Stone+ (tr); Science & Society Picture Library (tc). 6 Dorling Kindersley: Natural History Museum, London (ca). Getty Images: Siede Preis / Photodisc (bl). 7 Alamy Images: E D Torial (b). Dorling Kindersley: Natural History Museum, London (tl, cr). Getty Images: f8 Imaging / Hulton Archive (tr). 8–9 Science Photo Library: Dirk Wiersma (c). 10 Alamy Images: Tom Grundy (cl). Dorling Kindersley: Natural History Museum, London (br). 11 Dorling Kindersley: Natural History Museum, London (tl, br). 12 Dorling Kindersley: Natural History Museum, London (tc). 12–13 Dorling Kindersley: Natural History Museum, London (c). 14 Corbis: Frans Lanting. 15 Corbis: Atlantide Phototravel. 18 Dorling Kindersley: Oxford University Museum of Natural History (cl). 19 Dorling Kindersley: Natural History Museum, London (bl). 20 Dorling Kindersley: Natural History Museum, London (cl). 21 Corbis: Granville Harris / Eye Ubiquitous (tl). Getty Images: Jeff Foott / Discovery Channel Images (tc). 24–25 Dorling Kindersley: Natural History Museum, London (b). 28–29 Dreamstime.com: Natalia Bratslavsky. 30 Dorling Kindersley: Judith Miller / Freeman's (tl); Natural History Museum, London (bl, bl/Powdered Clay). 32 Dorling Kindersley: Natural History Museum, London (tl). 40–41 Alamy Images: Pritz / F1online digitale Bildagentur GmbH. 42 Dorling Kindersley: Rough Guides (tl). 50–51 Getty Images: Andreas Strauss / LOOK. 54 Dorling Kindersley: The Smithsonian Institution, Washington DC. 55 Dorling Kindersley: Judith Miller / 333 Auctions LLC. 56 Dorling Kindersley: Natural History Museum, London (c). 56–57 Alamy Images: Photoshot Holdings Ltd (b). 57 Dorling Kindersley: Natural History Museum, London (tl). 58 Dorling Kindersley: Natural History Museum, London (tl, br). 62 Dorling Kindersley: Oxford University Museum of Natural History (br). 63 Dorling Kindersley: Natural History Museum, London (tr). 65 Dorling Kindersley: Natural History Museum, London (c, br). 66 Dorling Kindersley: Natural History Museum, London (tl). 67 Corbis: Corbis Art (t). Dorling Kindersley: Natural History Museum, London (bc). Getty Images: Tim Graham (cr). 68 Dorling Kindersley: Natural History Museum, London (br); The Science Museum, London (cl). NASA: Human Spaceflight Collection (bl). 71 Dorling Kindersley: Oxford University Museum of Natural History (tr). 73 Dorling Kindersley: Natural History Museum, London (cl). 74–75 Getty Images: Radius Images. 76 Getty Images: Dea / A Dagli Orti (cl); Steve Eason / Hulton Archive (tl). 77 Dorling Kindersley: Natural History Museum London (cl). 88–89 Corbis: Peter Ginter / Science Faction. 90 Alamy Images: De Schuyter Marc / Arterra Picture Library (tl). Corbis: Macduff Everton (cl). SuperStock: imagebroker.net (bl). 92 Dorling Kindersley: Natural History Museum London (br). 102–103 Corbis: Bertrand Gardel / Hemis. 114–115 Corbis: Randy Faris. 119 Dorling Kindersley: Dan Bannister (tl). 122 Dorling Kindersley: Judith Miller / Blanchet et Associes (tl); Judith Miller / Sylvie Spectrum (cl); Judith Miller / Lynn & Brian Holmes (bl). 124 Dorling Kindersley: The Smithsonian Institution, Washington DC (tl). 127 Dorling Kindersley: Natural History Museum, London (tr). 132 Dorling Kindersley: Natural History Museum, London (tr). 141 Dorling Kindersley: Natural History Museum, London (tr). 142–143 Corbis: Jeff Daly / Visuals Unlimited.

Jacket images: *Front:* Dorling Kindersley: Natural History Museum, London fcrb, fcrb/ (Copper), c; *Spine:* Dorling Kindersley: Natural History Museum, London t.

All other images © Dorling Kindersley

For further information see: www.dkimages.com